UNDER THE TOTEM

UNDER THE TOTEM
In Search of a Path

Michael Eigen

KARNAC

First published in 2016 by
Karnac Books Ltd
118 Finchley Road
London NW3 5HT

British Library Cataloguing in Publication Data

A C.I.P. for this book is available from the British Library

ISBN-13: 978-1-78220-439-8

Typeset by V Publishing Solutions Pvt Ltd., Chennai, India

Printed in Great Britain by TJ International Ltd, Padstow, Cornwall

www.karnacbooks.com

ABOUT THE AUTHOR

Michael Eigen is a psychologist and psychoanalyst. He is Associate Clinical Professor of Psychology (adjunct) in the Postdoctoral Program in Psychotherapy and Psychoanalysis at New York University, and a Senior Member of the National Psychological Association for Psychoanalysis. He is the author of a number of books, including *Image, Sense, Infinities, and Everyday Life, Faith, The Birth of Experience*, and *Reshaping the Self: Reflections on Renewal Through Therapy*.

FOREWORD

Totem conveys spirit, a sense of the sacred. It has grown in meaning with usage, including a wide range of possibilities. It may be a representation of a plant or animal functioning as a symbol that binds a group together. It may include a group's relation to ancestors, mythic or actual. It may loosely refer to spiritual or creative aspects of experience, individual or group. Freud attempted to get under the symbol and define psychic forces and pressures that work below the surface. Jung opened further depths in exploration of the sacred, its meaning and function. Engagement with a sense of mystery that permeates existence continues today in many quarters, for example, art, music, religion, and depth psychologies.

Whether or not Freud's formulations are anthropologically valid is not the main issue here. I tend to see it as part of a field of encounter with the mystery of life that touches us in many ways. Some years ago, Alan Watts (1989) coined the phrase, "the taboo against knowing who you are." One likes to think of such a taboo as cultural but I suspect it is part and parcel of our nature, who we are. Culture reflects psychic life and vice versa. Kabbalah has a saying, "As above, so below; as below, so above." It seems also possible to say: as without, so within, as within, so without. A Zen master said, "Find where you are.

That's where practice begins." In the Bible God asks, "Where are you?" and a human being answers, "Here I am." It is this *here* that is at issue, eggs us to keep discovering more of ourselves, more of the universe. It seems the further we go, the more there is to go; no end to depths opening.

This book is an extended reverie, reflection, confession, assessment, engagement with psychic reality, a profound intertwining of multiple dimensions of our existence. Many schemas portray aspects of "worlds" we inhabit: nature, emotion–feeling, thought, intuition, spirit, and myriad experiences we have no names for. Aldous Huxley called us amphibian, at once material and spiritual, psychological and spiritual. Polis and psyche are part of each other. But these are raw and crude distinctions.

Distinctions we come up with can be helpful. We have built amazing physical and mental structures and continue building. Still, nothing we do exhausts the mystery of it all, within and without. Our jaw still drops and our heart dances when we see stars without and within. Words both obscure and create experience, depending on usage and possibility, but we keep digging in, letting go, feeling, starting over.

Under the totem are endless paths. In the Arthurian legends, each knight entered the forest in a different place, to find or create his path. We also do this beneath forests within, amazing unknown labyrinths under the surface, infinities everywhere in the finite, above–below, in–out. Some express this by saying we are made or carved out of infinity as well as matter and we can feel within our own experience mixtures of form and formlessness. Finite beings who breathe infinity.

My work is mainly about psychotherapy, psychoanalysis, one to one work with people. I have never felt the break between psychotherapy and spirituality many have. Psychotherapy spans all dimensions of life. Anything may enter a session and help or harm at a given moment. Mystery underlies it and there are different attitudes to mystery. It is not unusual to find that attitudes to mystery and oneself and others go together.

Bion (1970, 1994) does not use the word mystery, but privileges the unknown as a basic category of experience. We act as if we know ourselves, take ourselves for granted, yet what we take to be our identities are parts of unfathomable depths. A murderer may suppose that killing another will solve a problem only to discover that difficulties of being a psychical being continue and mount. One outlasts self-murders committed with or without awareness and wonders what the cause of persistent difficulties that having and being a self can be. Killing does not make one's problems go away. Would God have succeeded in obliterating disappointing humanity had he not saved Noah? God's wish reflects our own. The urge to obliterate difficulty, the difficulty of ourselves, is what we are up against, what we are working with, need to work with. Respect for the unknown and seemingly unsolvable difficulties of ourselves is a beginning.

Under the totem psyche is speaking. Can we hear and transmit it, to what extent, with what quality? Sometimes we imagine a phone rings and when we pick it up a voice says, "Hello, psyche speaking." "I'm listening," we say. A book can be a kind of phone ringing hoping to be picked up, heard, worked with, already the result of many conversations. Sometimes even hearing and working with a little bit can be helpful.

The method of this book is fragmentary. Different facets of experience emerge, recede, reappear; others come in. The emphasis is on feeling and imaginative reflection. There is a good deal drawn from therapy sessions and ongoing dialogues with workers who have touched my life personally or through public talks and writings, viz, Bion, Winnicott, Freud, Jung, Klein, Buber, Suzuki, Milner, Wittgenstein, Wertheimer, many others.

Among long-term personal therapists who have been important to me were Henry Elkin, Dorothy Bloch, and Michael

Kriegsfeld, all gone now. Early body work with Stanley Keleman has grown over the years. I wish to thank my ongoing Tuesday seminar, more than forty years old, mixtures of old and new colleagues. It has been a source of therapy for me all these years. We share a love of the psyche, its difficulties and gifts, what we sense and a vastness beyond sensing. I wish to thank a newer group, two or three years old, a Yahoo online work group made up of people from all over, much creative support, and questioning. It would take too long for all the thanks due to so many professional contacts that supported my growth, an immersion in depth psychological work affirming the human spirit for sixty years. But I can't resist mentioning a few names you might not otherwise hear, Mira Rothenberg, Mary Henle, Marie Coleman Nelson. Without my marriage and family, I would not have written a single book, nor would I have had the chance of learning the work of love so fully.

UNDER THE TOTEM
In Search of a Path

I once saw Anton Ehrenzweig (1971) speak on creativity. He mentioned staying up late so "the critic" gets sleepy and deeper dimensions of personality have more of a chance. Another way to get past the censor was by reading physicists, most of which he did not understand. He was intrigued by ideas and images about the universe. Terms fascinated him. He could almost sense what they were communicating. Something came through, although he might not be able to say what it was, a sense of fathoming something fathomless. He would go to sleep feeling nourished, as if making contact with the unknown, an opaque wonder that informed existence.

* * *

It is said that we fight over small differences. We fight over big ones too. Can we find another way to experience difference, train ourselves to be less belligerent? Sometimes I feel the human race is made of different species. Difference in sensibilities can seem so great. When I think of all the plant and animal forms I feel appreciative and wonder at the abundance of existence. I feel parallel appreciation of forms of artwork and creativity that are born from our efforts. I don't say this one or that is the truest or best but enjoy what each brings to life. There is

1

so much to gain by differences little or great. Agreement is not necessary for growth of impact and response. Where, then, do tyranny, rivalry, and power wars come from? Is it only a matter of territory, predator–prey, and survival need or a surplus of destructiveness from an unknown source within?

* * *

Wait in the unknown and further transformation will occur.

I have learned that from experience. How can I say it if destructiveness may be rooted in an unknown source within? The word wait and reality of waiting makes a difference.

This is something that psychoanalysis and aspects of meditation offer. Sitting with the destructive urge within rather than acting on it. Sitting as a different form of action. The dynamics of waiting in face of destructive pulls.

It is not only a matter of paying attention because attention comes and goes. It is more a matter of sitting through, waiting out. One may doze off and come back, become cloudy and vague punctuated by periods of attention. One attempts to stay with it but staying with it is intermittent. Freud noted that dreaming destructive things while asleep is safer than acting them out while awake. I wonder how much destruction while awake has a dreamlike quality, a kind of waking dream. Many qualities can feed destruction, including calculation, impulse, entitlement, injustice, pleasure and/or pain, determination, cunning, chance, opportunity, vindictiveness, hallucinatory holiness.

Psychoanalysis says, sit with them all. If you can, be with them, taste and smell experience. The more you sit with experience the more happens. Threads emerge and change, new feelings, thoughts, vantage points touch you. As time goes on, tolerance for experience builds, at least a little. One even develops a taste for tasting oneself and others and not settling for "this" view and no others.

It is not simply a matter of understanding. Socrates taught us that often what we take for knowledge is opinion. By sitting with inner waters we gradually make room for seeing how understanding can constrict us. Consciousness, our avenue of access and light of our lives, has its difficulties. What is it in us that seems to feel more or other than any of our capacities and informs them?

Waiting on the unknown and perhaps, as Levinas (Eigen, 2005) might say, the Impossible allows something else to happen. So much political psychology has been based on a control model, which involves inevitable swings between control and destructive outbreaks. What would a partnership model look like? Can we become better partners with our capacities and they with us? William Blake speaks of heaven as war in which each voice of personality has its maximum say yet all benefit. Rumi writes of welcoming all visitors within as valued guests. Here are hints of the richness of waiting on unknown transformational processes beyond control with which we partner.

* * *

How do we stop fighting with ourselves? Do we have to? Isn't fighting with ourselves part of growing? Can we tell the difference between destructive fighting and growth that can be part of fighting? Did the Holocaust produce growth? Does there have to be ghastly destruction for growth to occur or are there other ways to grow?

Rabbi Nachman asked why is it so difficult for some to meditate alone in the forest. He drew attention to the prevalence of fighting. Husband and wife fight as do parents and children and children with children. On a larger scale, nations fight and so do many groups. Alone in the forest, no one to fight with, one fights with oneself. Many tear themselves to shreds (Eigen, 2012).

3

The human race appears to lack a solution. A solution may not exist. Even so, sitting with insoluble problems can be growth producing.

* * *

One can learn a lot about ripping oneself to pieces. Learning to pay attention opens channels of experiencing. I think of Bodhidharma meditating in front of a wall for nine years (nine—time of birth). The story is of an external wall but I feel it as an internal wall. How do we grow by staying with inner walls? The wall may remain but *we* change. Perhaps we grow around it or it shrinks in importance. Something happens to us by facing our walls. Capacity to be with ourselves develops. *We* become more than the wall.

* * *

As a young man I learned that Buddhists are pacifists. As I learned more I became aware of wars between Buddhist sects and teachers, to the point of murdering one another. How can this be?

Pain and rivalry are part of life. Comparison mind inflames envy and lack. Nirvana offers a different perspective on sorrow but sorrow does not disappear. Was Buddha surprised about his disciples fighting or did he take it in stride, realizing the road was long and hard?

One can learn, to a degree, to bring up good feeling. At some point, something will upset it. There is something fundamental about going from good to bad feeling and bad to good and we need to learn how to be with it, at once absorbing it and developing a larger frame of reference.

It's not just rivalry between different people and groups but also rivalry between aspects of one's personality.

* * *

4

Professor Kenneth Setton, a scholar of medieval history, noted how barbarian invasions of the Roman Empire revitalized the latter (history class, University of Pennsylvania, 1955). War was destructive but also brought peoples together, creating intense interaction and mutual influence, which led to the spread of ideas and cultural possibilities.

I mentioned William Blake's vision of heaven being a constructive war in which no one is harmed and everyone is helped by maximum interchange of perspectives in which all voices have full say for the benefit of all. I used the term "constructive" but "creative" might be more apt—creative war. Intense interaction of all, mutually fertilizing all, "war" as fecundity. An ideal vision, certainly. Does anything like it exist on earth? Can it? Blake rightly calls it heaven.

The fact that we have a feeling that it could exist or should exist is telling. If only. Disappointment, disillusion, lack, insufficiency are important themes in psychoanalysis, partly under the rubric of the reality principle. Education to real living. Yet ideal feeling persists, sometimes as guide, surplus, glow, color, persecution (Eigen, 1993). Many writers have tried to reconcile ideal feeling and the hard facts of life and I often help patients by distinguishing between idealistic romantic and realistic love.

Winnicott (1992; see also Eigen, 1993) sought a new turn on the theme of destruction meeting environment. He depicted an infant's destructive fantasies outlasted by the environment he tries to destroy. The central case is of an infant's destructive tendency aimed at the mother who survives destruction without collapsing, retaliating, or inducing guilt. The environment survives the baby's feelings and survives them well enough, creating a sense of reality real in its own right and life affirming. Winnicott associates this moment with a sense of joy in the realness of being.

This is a pivotal experience. In therapy we learn how difficult it can be for a parent to take the baby's states and energy and work through them well. I recently saw a documentary of Kurt Cobain in which his mother could not take her child's energy and left the family to its devices. The child was a cauldron of creativity and disturbance which turned more and more into destructive creativity. He did not live till thirty. This is an extreme case with many complex known and unknown factors at work. Yet it brings out how problematic baby energy and states can be for a caregiver. One of my patients entered therapy because she found herself standing with a knife pointing at her baby, whose screams and discontent she could not take. We may idealize childhood but it is not easy for child or parent to get through and get through well.

I have been forced to somewhat modify Winnicott's formulation, which I think is at once real yet also an ideal. In reality I am deficient as a therapist. My responses often are mixed, miss the mark, inadequate. I have my own versions of collapse, retaliation, anxiety, shame, and guilt induction. Yet Winnicott's formulation has helped me and through me, many people I have worked with, with a slight shift of emphasis.

My emphasis tends to involve coming through. Over and over, we come through difficulties and mishaps of our personalities in particular situations. We survive ourselves, at times with decent quality. Therapy, as so much of life, is practice in survival and quality of survival. Coming through the muddle, at times the worst. It is an ancient model, destruction and rebuilding of the holy temple, death and resurrection, rebirth rituals.

It happens in daily life hour to hour. Now one is more dead, now more alive, different qualities of deadness and aliveness (Eigen, 1996). Sleeping and waking is another bit of the model. Beckett spoke of failing better. Coming through better. It may happen instantaneously but often takes a lot more time. *Waiting* and *staying with* are important. There is such a thing as creative waiting, a capacity that builds. I may die out in a session or mess up one or another way, but I come back. Next day, week, month and in some cases years. But that is what I do, my job. Regroup, come back, start over. A kind of stretched out rebirth over time or simply a process of being born that goes on all life long.

A result often is the patient is better able to come through too. An individual's sense of being able to die out and come back grows stronger. Life's setbacks are met with greater resourcefulness and equanimity, less rush towards quick, injurious "solutions," more ability to wait on possibility.

* * *

There are times when there is the need to act quickly, when only autonomic response will save the day. Bion wrote of the importance of the latter when under fire. Brain work is insufficient.

There are times when waiting on the unknown opens possibilities. Waiting on the Impossible opens possibilities. Find the unknown within you. Try not to wash it away. It will slip away on its own but you can make a gesture to evoke it. Things smoldering outside awareness sometimes pressure new birth. State of the unknown as a kind of fecund womb.

The *Lankavatara Sutra* (Eigen, 2011) speaks of transformations (Bion: T in O) going on in unknown Buddha lands. Transformational processes beyond concept, image, representation. Wait in the unknown and further transformation will occur. All the Buddhas that ever existed or will exist will come to your aid as transformational work goes on.

* * *

A rabbi asked, "Why do we sprinkle salt on challah to start the Sabbath?" He answered, "God, like salt, is invisible but flavors existence."

Rabbi Schneerson (1999) asked, "Why don't we see God?" And God answered, "If you cannot see Me it is not for My ethereality, it is because I am so real."

7

Reality too real to experience?

Bion said the therapist's resistance to the patient is because the patient is so real. He also said that resistance in general is resistance to the realness of reality. Resistance is part of reality. Reality can't be real without resisting itself. On a personality level, we should coin the term, *self-resistance*.

* * *

There are so many ways to experience a sense of depth. Sensing the real of unknown reality is one. Go to the state of the unknown. Find the unknown within you.

Can we say, "I am so real"? For Bion the unknown is so real, part of a sense of mystery that surrounds and permeates us. Can we say we don't see ourselves because we are so real?

Bion says we cannot know being but only be it. Can you see the being of existence? Feel it? You *are* it.

An ancient Hindu experience: Thou art that. Atman and Brahman are one. Or, if one wants to preserve identity, Atman ↔ Brahman, interwoven realities.

Merleau-Ponty writes that we are the universe aware of itself. Alan Watts that we are the universe "I'ing" itself.

We are all the more real because we are mostly unknown.

* * *

A rabbinic drosh (view, interpretation): The white of the Torah connotes God. White includes all color as God is inclusive. The black letters are we writing our lives, a process of formation. Black letters on white page are black flame on white flame. Black letters are on or above white underneath. A rabbinic saying: The Holy One decrees a decree and the tzaddik nullifies it.

Can you believe the tzaddik (sage, holy man) at that moment is above God? What a relationship we have with the Ultimate! God under us, supporting us as we develop.

A mundane analogue is time I spent in sessions with Wilfred Bion. When I met this big man, taller than me (I was forty-one, he eighty), I felt immediately that he was under me. It happened spontaneously, by itself. He placed himself under me, not artificially, but because that's who he was. It might have been the first time I came to deeply feel the word *understand* means to stand under.

Israel is called the servant of God. We serve Him because He serves us. There is no because. It just is. Another instance, Jesus as servant of man, to serve, save, humankind in love.

* * *

Early one morning, while driving to work, I thought I would have to go back home because I suddenly realized that I'd left my credit cards in my drawer. I had failed to take them with me and needed to pay for the garage and other items. After awhile it dawned on me I was still in bed and scheduled to do phone sessions from home. No need for credit cards and in any case they were in the drawer next to my bed and I was waking up.

The sense of needing credit cards I'd left at home was, in some way, more real than the reality of being in bed waking up, which startled me. I could relate the dream to returning to my childhood home where my life began, gone forever. The realness of the dream taps timeless childhood, the realness of memory—eternal time that was. One could, too, relate it to a sense of something missing, a sense that haunts life.

I think of the Taoist sage who dreamt he was a bird flying in the sky and now, awake, wonders if he is a bird dreaming he is a man walking on the ground. An actual state may feel less real than an imaginary state. Such is the power of mind.

Freud wrote of energy "cathecting" different inner or outer objects, making them feel especially real and significant, charged. Now one thing or state is filled with meaning or reality, now another. One can cathect or decathect some aspect of self or self as a whole. In this case, self varies along a spectrum of super-real to nonexistent. Subtle variations of softness–loudness and slow–fast tempos in music connect with variations of self–feeling. Nuances are myriad.

Robert Frost's response to speed reading was his wish to give a course on how to read more slowly. Slowing attention can open worlds that rapid attention may miss. My Husserl teacher in graduate school, Aaron Gurwitsch, read Husserl a sentence at a time, sometimes a phrase or word at a time. No speed reading here. It was like milking a cow in slow motion, slowly squeezing the milk of meaning out of the udders of words. The breast of words issues worlds of meaning.

At the time I was reading Freud's *An Outline of Psychoanalysis,* a highly condensed last work written in exile shortly before his death. I could only bear reading a sentence or two at a time. So many lines sent me to places without names. Dr. Gurwitsch's way of reading Husserl supported my slow reading of Freud, partly out of an incapacity to tolerate such buildup of intensity. A kind of slow dancing with great authors. We give permission to each other in so many unexpected ways.

* * *

I am not a fast writer. It feels like drawing water from a well. Slowly, sentences form. Where will they go? Freud said that when he began a sentence he didn't know how it would end. A kind of psychic slow motion. Sometimes I see colors and hear music when I write, as if words are colorful and musical. A word, a phrase, a sentence at a time. Mozart said he saw or heard or felt a symphony in a flash and had to translate it to notes. Einstein said he thought with vague images and muscular feels that later were translated mathematically.

Time fascinates us. So much time has been spent thinking and writing about and portraying or expressing time (dance, art, music …). Bion's *A Memoir of the Future,* Plato, Boethius, William Blake, Bergson, James Joyce, Einstein, science fiction, children's stories and games, time travel, time dimensions, spectrums of states. Simultaneity of eternity and time, separation. A mystical sense that there is nothing but God and everyday sense of individual time worlds. Different unconscious dimensions of time (Eigen, 1983).

A sentence at a time. Sense-tense (sentence), referring to meaning, time, and tension. Wordless tensions seek words, give birth to words. Many writers say they need to feel timelessness, as if they need to feel they have all the time in the world to write something. At the same time, they feel pressures to write, find the right words, and possibly, at times, a rush of words, mostly open to re-vision.

Timeless states and taking a walk with a child. You may have to get from here to there but the child gets lost in what she or he sees and hears. Sometimes it's like a sentence that doesn't know where it's going and doesn't have to know. It unfolds as it moves.

A desert guide once told my wife and me that a cactus would grow forever straight if not for wounds—it grows out from wounded places. Maybe this is a little like sentences growing out from knots of meaning. Freud wrote of "switch" words, like switches on tracks that change the direction of a train. Condensations of meaning can unravel like threads to pull, and each thread opens possibilities.

In *Toxic Nourishment* (1999, p. 206) I describe a walk with my then two-year-old son. He hangs on a gate swinging back and forth, tries to climb a wall but can't. I lift him and he walks on the wall, runs, topples, almost falls, laughs. Stairs catch his eye. I carry him off the wall and he climbs up and down the stairs until he sees a bird land nearby and runs after it. The bird flies away and lands close to where we started and he runs back after it. It flies away again and he sees the empty stroller (pushchair) near the stairs and wants to push it. We will never reach the end of the block unless he runs and makes me chase him. We were heading for the playground but the whole world beat us to it. The time-sense I feel is not a here to there kind of thing. It moves from thing-in-itself to thing-in-itself. Experience is

11

everything. I can feel impatience increasing in one system and a meditative state forming in another. For many, writing may not be like this, but for some it is.

* * *

Time, like the category of the hidden, has been explored by many. A mystic may feel there is nothing but God. Time is eternity and eternity time. Appreciation of spectrums of states, myriad beings, something special in each. Schools form around experiential nuclei.

Struggles with right–wrong and Rumi's field of meeting beyond them.

Contact beyond categories. To paraphrase: "Beyond right and wrong there is a field where we'll meet."

We hover in worlds of unknown intimacies, including intimacies with oneself. We tend the garden of life, the precious gift of experience. From the outside, it doesn't look like it felt from the inside. It's not a matter of finishing, of getting anyplace. The life of words, one word, phrase, one love at a time. All life in a word.

Have you ever spent time just looking at a word? Gazing and grazing, seeing where it takes you? I wonder how many people find themselves doing something like that, perhaps out of curiosity or wonder, or a spiritual exercise. Kabbalists are among those who did this with words, numbers, and colors. Gazing as dimensions of feeling and being open.

Lama Khouri wrote something nearly identical in a note to my Yahoo group, something that grew out of her own experience. "A sentence at a time—perhaps it also means faith. Faith that one will get there. This is what my children taught me. Going to the playground wasn't about going to the playground, it was about getting there. They would go up and down any staircase they found, climb on ledges, look at motor bikes. Getting to the bike was a sentence at a time."

12

I might modify her statement just a bit: Faith in the experience itself. Going, getting as elements of going into, getting into, being drawn into life experience itself.

* * *

People ask, faith in what? God, life, the cosmos? One might feel any of those at different times. Some people commit to one or the other and have strong belief systems to bolster them.

I've used the term, *psychoanalytic faith*. By that I don't mean faith in psychoanalysis. Any treatment may be better or worse, work sometimes in some ways and not in others. Years ago in the 1960s, therapists spoke about faith in the process. Process is a good word, but death and disease are processes too. Anything can go wrong at any moment.

Yet in sessions there is a difference between faith and cruel cynicism (not all cynicism is cruel), fidelity and betrayal. I have written about many sessions as crises of faith. Is life worth living? Why bother? One may be sunken, lost, beaten, not in a relative way but approaching absolute loss of faith. Something poisonous.

Anything one says is not quite it. Even dissolution, helplessness, and loss of faith can be part of a growth process. Faith beyond faith. Faith in face of loss of faith.

It is something more or else I can't pin down but very real in experience and consequence.

I sometimes feel wry jokes forming in me when people speak of faith in the cosmos. Destructiveness is inherent in cosmic work and even if necessary, not very comforting. The fact that I will die is basic and when I am told that my genes or books or dust live on, I laugh. Whatever they are, they are not me. Same with spirit, soul, or reincarnation. No consolation to me, though maybe for others. Death is obliteration. Why not take it on the chin? But then the creeping sense, maybe, just maybe ...

And yet the faith I mean persists in face of obliteration, cancellation, nullification. I can't explain it. I've heard the term blind faith, natural faith. I can see it working in animals. I can feel it in my body. But that is not exactly it either. It is a felt faith that runs through body, mind, psyche, spirit. It pervades existence, even in Holocausts, personal Holocausts. How is this possible? I don't know but I feel it. It is.

I have a cynical, sardonic side. Why not? It is helpful. Not just in contributing a balancing view but in seeing and experiencing facts of life. Adding a touch of another kind of transcendence, care, watchfulness, and honesty. In the 1960s when "basic trust" was in therapeutic vogue, R. D. Laing wrote of the value of basic mistrust. It is important to gain what one can from idealizing life and people and self, but it is also important to see through idealizations that stultify, mislead, and misshape.

I think of Jesus's counsel to his disciples: "Have hearts like a dove, brains like a serpent." Along this line, one day I asked my therapist about a Matisse drawing of a woman hanging on his wall. Her arms the shape of a heart around her torso while a slightly bemused semi-smile crossed her eyes and mouth. He said, "She wishes everyone well, but doesn't believe a word they say."

A paradoxical faith, simple and complex at the same time. "Render unto Caesar Caesar's, God God's." "The kingdom of heaven is within you." So is hell and purgatory and simple, everyday life, just plain me and more than me. Saint Paul was describing experiential reality when he said things like, "I yet not I, but God in me." Or states of grace in which boundaries between body, mind, spirit dissolve or are transcended or undercut.

Mystics affirm paradoxical states, personal and universal co-union (communion). Yet what I am trying to communicate is very simple, near, fluid, part of our psychic pores and cells.

14

I will have to pause, if not give up, look at you, sense you, and say, "It's really real. We're really real."

* * *

Can you feel the tears of life that touch the heart? The double meaning of tear as weeping and ripping.

I've heard some say there is a smile at the center of the heart. Heart is a term that can get pretty complicated. Hindus speak of two hearts, the impure one on the left, and the pure spiritual heart on the right. Jewish mysticism speaks of the evil inclination on the left side of the heart, good inclination on the right. Heart spans many dimensions, physical, emotional, soul hearts, spiritual heart. Sometimes there is a gut heart or a hara (below the navel) heart. For some thinkers head hearts. I wonder if great pianists have hand hearts. We speak of the great heart of a great athlete.

Heart can be anywhere. I heard Alexander Lowen speak of the heart–genital connection. Marion Milner spoke of consciousness in the big toe. I wonder if heart was there too. Is there heart in the Zen master's raised finger?

A sweet tear in the heart's smile.

* * *

Look what language does: ear in tear, hear, heart, fear, sear, dear, learn. How important hearing is. By using the couch, Freud tries to play down visual control, dominance, and mastery in order to touch a hearing–feeling dimension, between mastery and mystery.

Bion associates foundational emotional life with infinity, trying to open contact with domains deeper than defensive use of mastery (Bion, 1994; Eigen, 1979, 2012). Mastery–mystery paradox. We separate intertwined capacities. A sense of distinction–union permeates existence, separate–interwoven. Both poles feed our sense of being and self.

Throughout Freud's work, from beginning to end, there was a dialectic of fluidity–fixity. Libido, a fixed but fluid energy concept, was conceived in analogy with electricity and water. In later years, there was more emphasis on how the psyche was stuck, what blocked or stopped flow. There is a long history of looking at mind or psyche or consciousness and time as a flowing river and Freud re-translated this ancient, pervasive image into a kind of adaptation of energy from current physics, emphasizing the work energy does.

Another ancient image that is part of his conceptual nexus is the concept or sense of hiddenness. The hidden God, the hidden self, the hidden gate, hidden treasures, hidden intentions, hidden feeling, hidden worlds, hidden realities, hidden dimensions … one could go on: the category of the hidden. A theme in myth, fairy tales, spiritual–psychological discourse, childhood games, folk tales. The hidden—often allied with the unknown. We often hear how most of the matter in the universe is unknown. In one way or another it is a concept, an experience that runs through many aspects of life.

Freud uses many images and Bion many models. Say one thing, mean or find another. Say one thing, more swims into view. One could say that for Freud the deeper one goes, the more unknown. Bion emphasizes how unknown consciousness is as well. Both Freud and Bion write of a differentiated psyche growing from indistinguishable roots, perhaps drawing on a model of organismic growth. For Freud, an indescribable nether world between psyche and body, as if one moves through the mysterious dream navel into the unknowable. For Bion, unknowable reality, including the unknown emotional reality of sessions, signified by his notation, O (one of its meanings: Origin).

When thinking of Freud one wonders, which Freud? Freud the scientist, therapist, sage, dramatist? The formal or informal Freud. The formal Freud was strict in understanding his schemas as hypothetical constructs, educated suppositions, inferences. The informal Freud experienced them as living realities. For example, one of his last notes defines understanding mystical experience as the ego's apprehension or perception of the id. Id, ego, superego: for Freud at once hypothetical concepts and psychic realities.

Freud and his followers were often scored for reifying concepts, but I think the matter more complex and interesting. For Freud, as for Jung, Klein, WInnicott, and Bion, psyche is alive. Some may ask, does that make psychoanalysis akin to religion? Saint Paul: "It is a dreadful thing to fall into the hands of the living God." Might Freud or Jung say, at certain moments, "What a dreadful thing to fall into the hands of the living psyche?" Again, there are ways apparently distinct areas interweave, feed each other, make each other possible.

It was only a matter of time before psychoanalysis gravitated more and more towards an interest in psychotic and self-damaging processes, aliveness turned against itself, evolutionary challenges for humanity.

I'd like to say a special word for Freud the dramatist. Psychoanalysis is a confluence of a good number of influences, including physics, neurology, myth, and not the least, literature, especially drama. To what extent did ideas like the Oedipus complex or narcissism come from physics and neurology or from observation and reflection on human life and literature? Psychoanalysis as drama, conflicts between different aspects of personality very like tragedies of ancient Greece and, at times, biblical stories. Images and ideas drawn from sciences—neurology, biology, physics, archaeology—and the humanities fused. Freud came to think that immersion in the humanities might provide a better background for a psychoanalyst but he had the freedom to draw from what he felt significant across diverse fields.

Who knows to what extent everyday experience of "force" or philosophical ideas of energy formed the background for scientific reworking of these terms. Chi, prana, barakah, mana are some terms that form a background for a sense of vital power coursing through human affairs. Shifts of power in stories of ancient gods express shifts of states and affect dramas in multiple dimensions.

In high school, I remember terms like attraction–repulsion and "chemistry" were used to describe shifting currents of who liked who. Which came first, feelings and attempts to portray them or scientific definitions? Today they interpenetrate.

I could not avoid the sensation that, as I read Freud, libido had a cosmic as well as individual dimension. I could not avoid thinking, given his cocaine habit, that it might be, partly, a cocaine vision. Visionary experience and the hard thinking of science are not always at odds. Look how much Einstein emphasized imagination.

Freud drew many concepts from the physics of his day. Had he begun a little later, there would likely have been more field and less mechanical terms. Some of the concepts he applied to psychology include force, resistance, energy, work. He depicts a fixed energy system (although some energy is lost in the death drive, unexplained) undergoing transformations. Yet terms like force, attraction, repulsion, energy, and resistance are also drawn from how life feels, everyday experience. As mentioned above, a formal, "scientific" Freud and an implicitly informal aspect, in which psychological experience (e.g., feeling, sensation) gives rise to expressive language. To some extent, an experiential basis for the language of physics. One also wonders how the formal reshaping of terms and leaps of mathematics may, in turn, affect the way life is experienced.

Is there a poetry of science? Analogy and metaphor played a big role in Freud's thinking and writing. His thought mixes concepts and images drawn from physics, biology, archaeology, warfare, chemistry, neurology, psychology, world religion, mythology, and literature. His work is dramatic. He aims at psychic truth through what might be a grand fiction. There may be less a division between fact and fiction than is ordinarily surmised. Fable often conveys truth about life and feeling. When I was young I would hungrily read novels to learn about life. I would recognize portrayals of emotional truth. We would be poorer without all our fields of search. What I find in Freud is intense interaction between levels and domains of human experience. Freud the scientist, writer, therapist, and sage.

What did Freud and Jung share, above all? A sense of the living psyche. Both worked out a conceptual edifice. But underneath was a living reality. Freud would call his structural concepts "The Witch", his "metaphysics". Jung, too, was clear about the hypothetical nature of his constructs yet he lived them. They were felt realities. When Mrs. Jung was asked how her husband was doing she replied, "I don't know. He spends most of his time in the collective unconscious."

Something of this double attitude may have always been part of human capacity but I suspect it has intensified and developed with the passing of ages. Now it is increasingly possible to hold a lived reality in experience and investigate it at the same time. One feels the realness of life while remaining open to further thoughts and feelings. In a way, it is the end of dogma and a wedding of skepticism and faith.

Is the notation, *Ein Sof,* merely a notation or does it suggest something real? Bion's O is a notation for unknown reality. In the case of psychoanalysis, unknown, perhaps unknowable, emotional reality. And yet wasn't unknown reality real for Bion? For you?

There is an ethics of the unknown. An attitude of unknowing leaves things open, protects against false omniscience. In an argument with your partner you may be convinced that you are right, the other wrong. It is commonplace to blame the other, exonerate the self. The reverse also is not unusual. Aggression turns against the other and/or the self. If we assimilate the fact that we do not know everything about ourselves and the other and that, like the universe, we are mostly unknown to ourselves, a sense of humility and openness may have a chance to

19

grow. We may become more interested in learning more about who we are and readying for further development. This is an entirely different attitude than slamming the door with dogma.

The possibility of a more exploratory appreciation of complexity is an old concern. Socrates taught that much of what passes for knowledge is opinion and that we are victimized by our self-celebratory tendencies. In my book, *Rage* (2001b), I write that the sense of being "right" has done more harm in human history than any other attitude. It is even used to justify murder. Self-idolatry goes deep and it is hard to break out of the right–wrong trap.

Jesus and Rumi come at it from somewhat different directions but profoundly converge. Jesus: Forgive them, they don't know what they're doing. Rumi: Beyond right and wrong there is a field. I will meet you there.

Eddington: Something unknown is doing we don't know what.

Both Moses and Freud end with a question. Moses: Will good or evil win? Freud: Will the life drive or death drive win?

And what are our questions? It is said the answer is the death of the question. But what we call answers are just beginnings. When someone asks a question in a workshop, I may say I can't answer it but can try to respond. A response can open and close psychic reality. With luck, goodwill, persistence, and care (not to mention skill and experience), mutual fields of impact-response grow.

* * *

A patient felt angry and hurt by my asking questions she could not answer. I easily see how irritating I can be. Both of us can be pretty irritating. Her response made me rethink mine. What was I doing wrong? Am I doing anything right? And what would that look like? Again, trapped by right and wrong.

What do I mean when I ask a question? One of my teachers years ago taught not to ask a question you don't know the answer to. She was thinking in terms of the formula what, how, why. What: descriptive level; How: dynamic level; Why: etiology. Another part of this was the formula: analyze defense before drive. Defense analysis formed a major part of the work. One never knows what's under a defense or what purposes it fulfills, so carefulness is in order.

As time went on I discovered that "what" is not so easy and to know "how" and "why" can be pretty presumptuous. One guesses, constructs, tries out. The whole enterprise is more hypothesis making than answering. Makes me wonder what my teacher knew or *thought* she knew. To *think* one knows something and to be aware it is one's thought process one is observing opens a gate to further possibilities. It is not clear that knowing or knowledge is the main thing at stake so much as open-ended exploring, asking.

It gradually dawned on me that questions I was asking patients were questions I was asking myself as well. A journey of inquiry opening more fields of inquiry. A sojourn that first seems daunting and overwhelming but also is beautiful.

At some point, I was able to say, "When I ask questions, I don't expect you (or I) to 'know'. I mean then to help evoke more reverie or fantasy or memory or thinking, imagining, feeling, willing—more free associations, more psychic life … If they shut you down rather than lead you to say or open more, or explore and experiment, then they fail in their purpose."

I added something I felt might be too much pressure, too pushy, but took the chance: "Maybe we can learn more what they [questions] do … frustrate, anger you?"

She seemed to think I was accusing her of something and felt she must be frustrating me. She asked how frustrating was she for me, how angry did she make me?

So maybe we can investigate how angry we made each other.

At the same time I felt something deeper, a sense of loss as to what to do. I said so and added, "We may have reached the limits of what I can do. I can and do try to listen and respond but my responses are inadequate."

Her first reaction was fear and anger—was I telling her our therapy was over, that I could not work with her, that I wanted to get rid of her?

"No," I responded. "That didn't occur to me. I was feeling inadequate, at a loss how to be, sad I may not be good enough for the job." As soon as the words were out of my mouth I felt, who is good enough? Good enough is not the issue. We are what we are, frail mortals together, doing what we can. The loss I felt was without end. It was for unborn capacity.

* * *

There has always been one or another form of human therapy. Evidence suggests this was so when we lived in caves. People have been trying to cure physical and mental pain from time immemorial. Since ancient and perhaps pre-ancient times there have been healers.

I think psychoanalysis makes a contribution, adds to the pool, by calling attention to psychic realities, touching details of what goes on within oneself and between patient and therapist, new forms of interaction. I don't know that there previously existed such a nuanced sense of self–other interweaving and exploration, experiencing experience and investigating it as it happens moment to moment and over time, hot off the psyche. Wordsworth's "emotion recollected in tranquility" might be a hint, but he was referring to the poet's relationship to himself and his writing. In therapy we have co-creative partners discovering tastes of relationships with ourselves and others in vivo. Harold Bloom outra-geously claimed Shakespeare invented the "human" as we know it. I'm tempted to claim Freud invented the psyche (a term from antiquity). Or, at least, ways of apprehend-ing psychic life with additional color, flavor, scent, and significance.

22

Bion feels that psychoanalysis is embryonic and that there is an embryonic aspect of the human psyche. There have been proliferations of "schools" of psychoanalysis and psychoanalytically related, derived, or informed therapies. New movements continue to this moment. I have gained from all of them that I have had contact with. I feel wars between groups is more territorial and political or economic than knowledge based. Parochial wars are based on narrowing the field of possible knowledge to sectors that have been carved out, hands on the elephant. We may not know how they fit together or are mutually nourishing. But that does not nullify positive contributions each can make. No matter what claims one makes, psychotherapy involves sensing and feeling one's way into work with oneself and another with difficulties and roadblocks. There is no problem-free environment, inner or outer, for human beings.

Uncertainty is so much a part of this work that Bion called the psychoanalytic attitude Faith, which he, partly, described as being without memory, expectation, desire, or understanding. Radical openness to present impact and response. He would say if you think you're seeing the same person, you're seeing the wrong person. At times, he would say that about changes from moment to moment in the session itself. What changes have you and the patient undergone since the latter entered the room? Can one ever catch up to the "what"? One works with the uncatchable. Notations Bion used for this situation: F in O; T in O. Faith in face of unknown reality. Transformations in unknown reality. To paraphrase a Bion saying, it's not a matter of knowing O but being O (Eigen, 1993, p. 124; 1998, 2012).

This is a far cry from words in psychoanalytic institute catalogues emphasizing understanding. It is much closer to Freud's "free-floating attention" and "free association". Neither may be "free" but an open attitudinal direction is set as a challenge. Surely there is growth in understanding but something more, deeper, fuller, harder to pin down linked with quality of experiencing, a feel for life (Eigen, 2004, 2007). It seems safe to say no one is without expectation, memory, understanding, and desire. Bion describes an impossibility as the path of psychoanalysis. In one's own way one senses the possibility of a shift of attitude and emphasis, a field of practice, a path of growth. In particular, growth of a capacity Bion points to. Bion's work is an avenue of access and aid to cultivating the openness to experiencing he touches. To accept this challenge is a humbling act of respect and care for psychic reality that necessarily requires leaving room for the unknown in others and oneself.

In my experience, I reached a deep point of not knowing towards the end of the sequence with my patient; whereas, my patient felt I was reproaching her (the end of the preceding section). We reached a moment of divide yet potential rapport. As well as mistrust and criticism, I suspect she sensed something in my helplessness waiting on something further, not just rejection. This waiting for something is also an invitation to creativity, continuity across a void.

* * *

I'm aware there is a time to act, a time to wait. *Ecclesiastes* and the *I Ching* are classic manuals on changing seasons. When to hide, when to hit. There is a difference between acting in self-defense or a just cause and preemptively starting a war. In our culture, waiting is seen as weakness. We've come a long way from John Milton's "They also serve who only stand and wait" ("On His Blindness", 1673). When I was young and read this poem I thanked Milton and wept. He communicated profound, sonorous goodness coming through strife and hardship and haste, a communication made from one soul to another across centuries.

We associate blindness with wisdom but also with rashness, thoughtlessness. Words work hard to mean so much. We qualify one statement with another, travel through labyrinths of meaning. If I speak of the wisdom of waiting, I already hear someone speak of its impudent imprudence. Mind is crowded. Inner crows attack from all directions.

Wonderful paintings of Buddha sitting still as demons and apparitions attack and are pacified. Freud speaks of a still point in the midst of psychotic tumult, an observer in the storm. For some, a still point of the soul, Sabbath point of personality, a creative aspect of waiting, birthplace of unexpected experiencing (Eigen, 2005).

* * *

We are hardwired for danger. Almost every system we have is primed to react to danger. We may view something in focal vision but if something unexpectedly crosses peripheral vision we immediately give it attention, checking for danger.

So many people have trouble sleeping for so many reasons. But we are never fully asleep. While one part of the brain sleeps, another stands guard, awake, ready to respond to danger. Sometimes vigilance mushrooms.

In one case, a seer, spiritual healer, teacher of yoga, meditation, breathing, and related arts came for help with a whirring mind that would not let her sleep. Spirits visit her and she can give information to seekers about those who have passed away. A caring woman living a full life, a grandmother in an enduring marriage with all its vicissitudes.

She seeks help because sleep problems worsened and she is up days at a time and it is taking a toll. She recalls in early childhood being terrified of the night because of horrible nightmares. It is hard to describe the mixture of assurance, calm, balance, and fright, as if some sector of her being has a good enough inner object to help balance internal attacks, and another sector does not and attacks prevail, alarmingly so, threatening her health. It is as if systems that search and are alert for danger are working overtime. The watchman triggers terror and terror overthrows the watcher.

"I thought I outgrew my childhood terrors. They faded over time." Rose (a name I'm adopting here) remained quiet for a time. "I used to be afraid our house was haunted and buried myself under the covers in dread. Spirits could be anywhere, only then I called them ghosts. It never occurred to me that *I* was the haunted house. Room after room filled with fright.

"I saw an old movie of a haunted mansion and I had to hide my eyes when a door was opened to another room. What horror would be there? School was hard for me in many ways but a relief. I could pour myself into work with real people all around me. The ghost world lessened, even disappeared for awhile. The closer I got to home the more afraid I became. Would I find my mother dead on the floor, killed by an evil spirit?"

"So often a child going off to school is afraid mother won't be there on return, but this is a more dramatic version of fear of abandonment. Murder by unknown, unstoppable forces."

"Yes," she responded to my gesture. "Unknown, unstoppable force—that's just what I felt. I didn't know what it was but ..."

"More real than the seen world ..."

"Yes, but when I was with others, playing, running, it faded."

"Two worlds."

"And both were real. *Are* real. People talked about the outside world but not much, if anything, about inside worlds. I was left to myself with them."

"Not something school focuses on or knows what to do with."

"Does anyone?" Rose asked. "I thought I found an answer when I was older, meditation, yoga, channeling. A way of making use of a talent, a gift. And now it's back worse than ever. No, not worse than ever, but it feels like that because I've been OK so long. It's like unfinished business has come back to haunt me."

"The gate that opens and closes can't close."

"Two years ago I began medication and it helped, not completely, but relief. Then the sleeplessness started and my doctor suggested I speak with you."

"Are you ready for a therapy journey?"

"It's a relief to be here, ready or not. I feel I can say almost anything. I feel you listening. Maybe you are kind of channeling too. It's familiar being here. I get the idea that ghosts will find a home."

Freud made a catalogue of internal danger signals, anxiety, shame, guilt among them. He labeled many kinds of anxiety, for example, birth anxiety, separation and abandonment anxieties, castration anxiety. Since Freud the list has expanded. One thing psychoanalysis finds is that we are phobic about our own minds. We can posit other worlds but a lot can be gained by associating fears in the night with mental dread. Our minds or psyches or souls populate boundless, amorphous night with what we put in people during the day. We are a repository of age-old trauma, catastrophic happenings and fears. Good feeling competes with bad, a balance that shifts and sometimes places us in jeopardy. One thing therapy can do, depending on luck, circumstance, and skill, is shift the balance for the better. Even a little can go a long way.

* * *

Lacan writes of the unconscious opening and closing, pulsations of a "slit". William Blake compares creative moments in time to pulsations of an artery. My words to Rose, the gate that opens and closes can't close, touches this rhythm, a deep rhythm in our beings, not the only rhythm but important, like breathing and pulse (Eigen, 2004).

Lacan's image feels vaginal to me, a little clitoral too. Pulsations of the slit. The unconscious subject speaking, communication in the depths, psyche speaking. Can you feel the pulse, hear the voice? A still small voice, thunder? A voice of anguish, throbs, wounds, yearning? Joy that obliterates existence?

Psyche speaking. Rose can't shut it out. She can stop listening but can't stop hearing. Visitations spiraling, gone wild, finding her at their mercy, finding an opening and pouring through.

Bion speaks of a contact barrier linking unconscious–conscious communication, slowing it down, speeding it up, between flooding and nothingness. How do we communicate with ourselves? In Rose's case, what is missing?

There are ways the psyche needs to resist itself, modulate its pace. In some instances, the psyche may be missing or out of play. I got a sense that Rose skipped steps, jumped levels, went straight to spirit without enough of a psychic bridge. Does it sound strange to say that the psyche as bridge between dimensions provides accelerating–braking rhythms? What was Rose skipping over, reaching for? It was as if she was trying to go straight to the source while skipping over the psyche. The pulse of the psyche bleeding, grieving, gasping, furious, hoping. Fear transferred from flesh to spirit at a loss of psychic density.

After working for some time I found myself saying, "You jumped to the goal region to avoid the journey?" Substituting dreads of spirit for dreads of psyche?

"I thought it made me special. I accessed worlds others couldn't. I was something more, a guide."

"But you wonder now how much you left yourself behind?"

"I was there, living fully, but fear mounted and I couldn't sleep. Am I afraid I will find myself in my sleep and won't be able to take it?"

"Maybe we can build a bridge between levels …"

"And fill myself out more …?"

Another time she asked, "With more me, will the spirit worlds vanish? Will too much me shut them out?"

"A real fear," I said. "But maybe with a little more you, the gate will open and close better."

How much psyche do we skip over in order to live?

* * *

In my twenties I began saying "I love you" when alone going to sleep. The words would bubble up I never knew when. They would come up, I love you, I love you. Who was I saying this to? A missing partner? God? Who was speaking? Was someone saying that to me?

The words sounded like my voice, voiceless in the darkness, silent words in the darkness of night. Because I was lonely? Did they soothe? They would fill my body and soul and heal.

It is now nearly sixty years later and the words still come when I am going to sleep. Not every night but when they remember. My wife is asleep next to me. My children are grown. I am nearing the end. The darkness is welcoming. "I love you, I love you." Are they coming from my heart? No place at all? Where are they going? Who is speaking? Who is hearing? From darkness to darkness? Tears begin to form. I love you, love you. Love.

* * *

A quality not ordinarily associated with Bion, or perhaps not made explicit enough, is his supportiveness in face of the diversity of psychic states. Supporting the psyche to better tolerate, whatever extent possible, the life of the psyche, life that threatens and enriches. In a way, the psyche is its own worse threat and needs support in face of itself. This by no means ignores threats from outside but does bring into view special difficulties we face with regard to our own makeup. It was perhaps an astonishing formulation he made, calling Faith the psychoanalytic attitude, characterized by radical openness in face of emotional reality. Lack of resources in face of internal (not only external) catastrophe is an evolutionary challenge for the human race.

* * *

In *Coming Through the Whirlwind* (Eigen, 1992), half the book is about an attractive woman who tended to sleep with ministers of churches she attended. I could feel the pull in sessions and had to maintain the tension of affirming sexuality while engaging her in what her psyche was trying to accomplish with it. Sex, we know, is often not just sex but carries a great load as an ego machine. And, at very early levels, can be associated with nursing—sex as nursing, psychophysical nourishment, at once trying to make up for deficiencies while adding experiential richness. For this particular person, it was also a way to get closer to God. Nearer one way, farther another, as fulfillment and guilt commingled. A barrier could not quite be bridged.

I looked forward to the end of sessions when we touched hands goodbye, an electric thrill. There is a tension in therapy that is unavoidable as sexual urges are affirmed without acting them out literally in sessions. But that is no different than withstanding the pull of sexual urges in raising children, affirming feeling while respecting persons. It is part of a frustration built into life, a sacrifice we willingly make for a greater good.

Something similar happens in Winnicott's "use of object" formulation (Eigen, 1993, 2014c). The infant's destructive feelings become life affirming depending on responses they meet. In meeting them, the mother affirms the baby's urge to life without allowing herself to be hurt. A tension is built into experience which, if grown into well through time and repetition, promotes growth as a fuller person.

At the same time, we may sense ways our psyche is stunted, warped, in some way disabled, and left behind. We may sense deficiencies without being able to say or know what they are.

Many live as partial psychic amputees, making use of what we can, certainly a ground for universal compassion.

* * *

Someone asked if I thought there was a universal "psychotic core" (Eigen, 1986). I don't know if I have a clear position. I try to adapt formulations to particular situations and contexts. I do feel operations that could be called psychotic tend to be widespread in humanity and that it is an evolutionary challenge to become aware of them, meet them, and begin a digestion process so that we become less destructive and self-destructive, insofar as that is possible.

I do believe such operations span what is called normal, psychotic, borderline, narcissistic, and neurotic. I remember Henry Elkin saying in a seminar, "Behind every neurosis is a hidden psychosis." We have no way of knowing if that is true or not or in what ways it might be true. But it seems to me to be very worth meditating on. What is called "normal" is not always so "sane."

Another consideration is reversible states. Freud wrote of a witness or observer during a psychotic storm. A small, still space within, perhaps an eye of the hurricane or a third eye. He felt someday psychosis could be worked with, pointing to immense changes of states occurring in day and night, waking consciousness and dream life. He reasoned if such states could reverse or follow one another in everyday life, why couldn't psychotic and other states oscillate or reverse?

Perhaps that might parallel a possibility of highly anxious states changing into more peaceful states. This leaves out considerations that aspects of psychic life might be deformed, and simple reversal or popping back into better shape has formidable obstacles. Nevertheless, there are instances of enormous shifts between worse and better states, including the reality of momentous transformation processes. Much therapeutic work is not as dramatic, working with difficulties a little at a time.

31

However, sometimes I do feel we work with the Impossible or Unbearable or Intolerable in possible, bearable, tolerable doses.

* * *

So often acute change is emphasized in transformational processes. Phrases like born again, twice born, disruption of homeostasis are allied with radical change. Bion has a vocabulary of turbulence and catastrophic change but also patience, sticking with slow grinding out of movement that may not be noticeable for some time, building tolerance and sensitivity to nuances, small as well as large changes.

There is no wonder that acute and radical change is often emphasized. The unfolding stages of an embryo evoke in me appreciative awe beyond belief. Picture an adult going through the radical growth an embryo-fetus does. What is it going through? How can it take it? My jaw drops in absolute wonder. I don't think most of us could stand doing it. Even in childhood my mother tried to console me by speaking of growing pains.

Storms, earthquakes, tsunamis, big and little bangs, deserts, tundras, black winters, enormous shifts in climate, wars, death, mutilation, violence of all stripes, not to mention arrays of self-injury, not just falling off a cliff but tripping on one's own feet, biting one's mouth. Pain from within and without. The mystery of destructive pleasures, confusion, and bafflement of joys that land us in hell, turning us inside out, making us ask where are we, who are we?

No wonder we seek refuge in slow processes, gradual aspects of life. Science speaks of explosive and cooling processes, terms that perhaps were taken from daily life, such as temper fits and cooling off. A lot of language we use unconsciously refers to internal affect dramas that are part of the background of living, the play of moods. Emotional temperature varies throughout the day. I suspect the Bible places so much emphasis on peace because there is so little of it. People even use it as a form of greeting—shalom, salaam—a hope more than reality.

Mystics speak of a peace that passes understanding, profound peace below the storm. When I was a child I wondered if that had something to do with our lack of presence before birth and after death. The blank peace of not being there when so much was/is/will be going on. Now I also think it a more positive reality, a real dimension that is part of life.

As we grow more comfortable thinking–experiencing in terms of multidimensionality and complexity, there is violent backlash towards simplification: beheadings, burnings, shootings in God's name or in the name of a "cause" or ideal. Our way or the highway. Varied strands of tendencies are played out in the social scene, from family to state to global interaction. One or another way, this has always been so. Forms and virulence vary but many psychic ingredients have remained constant. One persistent theme, for example, involves attitudes rotating around parochial–universal modes of acceptance (letting in) and rejection (exclusion). We are appalled by news reports today of human groups treating other groups as subhuman, fit for evacuation. In many situations it is hard to say what is change or resistance to change and what each may mean to a given subculture.

Nevertheless, I would like to say a word for gradual change and repetition. We know from childhood how important and enriching repetition can be. Hearing the same stories, having the same parents and siblings and relatives. Going to sleep at night, waking up at day. Breathing, eating, opening and closing one's eyes, familiar sounds, scents, and touch. Not to mention the sameness of being on planet earth, one planet shared by all. Or perhaps I should say, shared and fought over by all.

Repetition is often put down but its values are many. Going over something not only deepens and enriches but opens further gates of experience, often in subtle ways. Gentle change can be as important as violent change. Tenderness can open dimensions of experience that brings life to places one never expected, making it worthwhile in ways one never dreamt. When discussing repetitive dreams, Gregory Bateson somewhere remarked that they are not repetitive without valuable, if subtle differences. Repetition does not always mean "same." Bateson spoke of "news of difference" that slight variations in repetitive dreams can bring. One can apply this observation to much experience.

I've suggested to many people to feel their breathing. Not necessarily any strict "mindfulness," "observing," although that is possible. Just sit or lay down or walk or whatever position and feel your breathing. So much feeling is attached to breathing. I never tire of it. Pores, cells, and organs I didn't know existed—one feels differently all through one's body, one's being. Over time, many are surprised how much wealth is hidden in the most common functions. I can imagine what the Zen master who lifts one finger may feel, whether rising in slow motion or a micro-moment. One finger Zen—inexhaustible.

I mentioned earlier how falling asleep can be a very special time. I've coached many to allow sensitivity to such a time open possibilities of experience. Little by little, new pathways grow, sensitivity to life blossoms. In time, this transfers to appreciation of how it feels to walk down a street or sit by a river or feel the lift a passing glance from a smiling face can bring. I'm a believer in little moments unanticipated gentleness can bring.

When meditating on this passage I thought of everything my wife and I have gone through. It was a late marriage, I in my forties, she thirties, and what haven't we experienced, Apollonian–Dionysian and beyond. We broke up many times before taking the leap. The whole spectrum of emotions have been our guests and we theirs. We learn that one set of affective attitudes does not preclude another. All have a say, a place, add to the color and challenge.

Relationships are not easy. Nor is being alone. Being a human being is necessarily fraught with impossibility. The Impossible gives birth to possibilities.

Marriage or partnership, whatever upheavals, also participates in the category of repetition and familiarity (family). Whatever the strangeness and difficulties, it is the "same" person you are sharing your life with, lying in bed with, waking up with. The Atlantic Ocean not far from our house has been the Atlantic Ocean for a long time, but it is not the same today as yesterday, this hour as last hour. But we know where it is and can go there, walk along the water, dip, dry, marvel at the colors around and inside us. Many shorter relationships played a role in learning about life, but this unanticipated thirty-five years together is something else. Almost eighty years old, domains of love I could not have known about bring tears of appreciation.

* * *

Repetition plays a role in familiarity and growth in countless ways. Small changes add up. I recently heard of a study in which repetitious physical activity, in this case on a stationary exercise bike, led to growth of white matter in the brain for both schizophrenic and "normal" subjects. The next time I went running after hearing this news I thought how comforting and life sustaining repetitious behavior can be. I felt my body's rhythmic repetition block after block in the sunlight, a music of the body. Once in the park, familiar sounds of weekend drums added to the pulse. No wonder ancients heard music of the spheres. And we explore music (or cacophony) of the psyche. Existence is musical. My body's pace and feel automatically adapted to the drumming, and running became easier.

Repetitious behaviors are among our favorite pleasures. Perhaps certain repetitious behaviors are so rewarding exactly because survival requires them. OK—not always so rewarding. There were times during my run I had to push to keep going, past resistances, pains, fatigue, fear of injury. Slow down, speed up, zigzag, breathe a little differently, feel various parts of my body complaining or sustaining. Still, a good part felt OK and sometimes better. Nearing the hour and a half mark, a wall I didn't know was there lifted and little heavens gently suffused different areas, muted ecstasies of movement. I think of Rabbi Nachman who is said to have danced so slowly you couldn't see him move (Eigen, 2012). The stillness of running.

* * *

Freud emphasized negative repetitious patterns ("repetition compulsion"), states and behaviors deleterious to self–other. As usual, doubleness, repetition as useful and more than useful and repetition as destructive. A positive function of repetition is the role it plays in learning and creativity. Repetition and the new are not necessarily enemies. They can be co-nourishing. Nevertheless, destructive patterns of repetition play an enormous role in human life.

People often speak of "bad habits" as forms of addiction. Compulsive behavior ranges from the trivial to acts that can destroy a life. All kinds of therapy have grown up in attempting to help individuals with variable results. Similarly, how do we address destructive behavior of societies? In some ways, psychoanalysis is a meditation on destructive urges. At least the problem is noted, focused on, questioned. Many people have been helped but the global problem remains immense.

* * *

Individuals often have divided up activities and states and pitted one against the other. Either you are more conservative, tied to the past, or more progressive, promoting change. That the two go together, symbiotic, does not seem to satisfy an athletic need for competition. Bergson (1911) noted the importance of both in creative evolution and Bion (1970) amplified tensions between the mystic and the group. Who knows, with a little more white matter gained through repetition, something of a new idea or feeling or state of being might begin to form. Or perhaps the repetition in itself is rewarding for its own sake.

* * *

Wertheimer (1940) moves the discussion of freedom away from free will to qualities of experience, for example, moments one feels more free or blocked. One moment an outfielder is fluid, makes an impossible catch. The next moment, tied in knots, unable to do anything right. I've written about the former as an alpha function moment, the latter a beta knot (Eigen, 2004). Moments of feeling free come and go. Wertheimer feels freedom is, in part, an attitude.

One day, while running around the park, I heard a young mother running with a dog on a leash, screaming (with pleasure, fun, hardship?), "Max, Max, slow down, I can't keep up with you." In back of the mother was a little girl on a little two-wheel bike with a delighted face. Was the mother playing a game? Max led the parade, trying to run with all his might, tugging at the leash, the mother trying to keep up, the girl cheering him on. At a peak moment, Max outran the shrieking mother, "Max! Max! You're going too fast" to the delight of the little girl who shouted, "Max is happy. Max is happy." The dog couldn't believe his luck, running nearly as fast as he could on the park road, muscles glistening, legs extended. The mother was forced to stop and hold Max back. The three stood still for moments to regroup, then started up again, the mother setting a slower pace, holding the leash more tightly, Max and the little girl tagging along, adapting. Everyone was OK enough. I trotted by, for the moment feeling Max's happy moment in myself.

* * *

Ashis Roy wrote in a note to my Yahoo group: "It reminds me of being able to cycle as a kid with my head turned towards the sky and feeling truly free and independent." Such moments of joy remain as points of reference in the background of life, oscillating, linking, contrasting, fusing with the pain of life.

James Tyler Carpenter sent this George Bernard Shaw quote, "As long as one has skeletons in the closet, one might as well make them dance." In the mood I'm trying to convey here I couldn't help responding, "Make them? They're not dancing already?"

As Chogyam Trungpa once said to a friend of mine, "Look again!"

Or a Hafiz line Robin Bagai sent: "I know the way you can get/When you have not had a drink of Love."

Words that came to me in response: "The ocean outside is wondrous/The ocean within even more wondrous."

Keats: "A thing of beauty is a joy forever."

Some say the earth will be gone and Shakespeare and Homer as if they never existed. Yet this living moment is forever now, a precious instant.

* * *

Emptiness and plenitude are experiences that have been with us since antiquity. The birth of symbols has been attributed to both. Objects of everyday life express emotional realities. My cup is empty; my cup runneth over. A seamless fit between external and internal reality.

In a story of beginnings the Bible tells of void, chaos, abundance—all significant parts of experience, in this instance, creative experience. In psychoanalysis, Marion Milner emphasizes expressive overflow in the rise of affective symbols. Lacan and Bion tend to emphasize absence, gap, caesura. To my mind, both states intertwine, form a spectrum of possibility.

They play a role in the history of science. Newton hypothesized empty space and supposed that God held it all together. Field theory wrote of filled space in which forces could work at a distance. Filled and empty are basic categories of experience.

Bion depicted an emotional element in perception of filled–empty, the infant's movement between empty–filled in the feeding situation. Not just food but rise and fall of emotion, now more filled with feeling, now emptier. The Psalms dramatically portray states of empty–full depending on God's presence–absence, emotional dramas centered around what Elkin (1972) calls primordial Self and Other.

Gestalt psychology, a field theory, notes force fields in emotional–motivational dimensions, including perceived gaps between self and world, self and self, and pressures exerted by gaps in knowledge, a cognitive component linked with affect. Mary Henle (1962) described different kinds of gaps in knowledge as part of the push and pull of force fields giving rise to ideas. One can say the same for feelings too.

In psychoanalysis, Lacan is well known for emphasis on a constitutive gap in the psyche. Attempts to fill structural gaps often are delusional, imaginary, even psychotic, although one may try to symbolically re-present them (Eigen, 1993).

One could develop a nosology of gaps emphasizing how they feel and function. There are all sorts of gaps, soft, hard, different shapes and sizes and textures. Friendly gaps, hostile, freeing, swallowing, uplifting, terrifying, protective, permitting. A wound may be a gap or perforation around which parts of personality calcify. Bion speaks of oversaturated spaces, such as oversaturated with meaning. He likes leaving room for more to develop. One can conceive of a spectrum of less–more saturated dimensions with varied nuances.

Buber and Winnicott emphasize "between".

Freud's notion of condensation, by contrast, opens rich possibilities of things meshed together, compressed.

Variations by many thinkers on the enduring theme of empty–full continue to this day.

* * *

Here are some variations posted by online group members.

Marlene Goldsmith

"I've always thought that silence runs in, through, and around the poetic word, sometimes foreground and complete, sometimes submerged in the word, sometimes washing into the background.

"I see silence and words/sounds as intimately involved and part of one another. The poem for me has always emerged from and then dissolved back into silence. Without its resonating sounds we wouldn't have that beautiful stillness afterwards (and vice versa). In part, the rhythmic placing of words in a poem allows us to 'hear' and feel the silence that runs through poetry."

Jeffrey Eaton

"A space between two thoughts, between two breaths, between two instants, can open the recognition of the difference between being elsewhere and being 'now–here'. As we discover the now–here (I/thou) experience, the elsewhere of images fades to the background. As the I/thou expands, then I/thou become one, no separation. Here is the paradox of caesura as gap/connection. Connection is actually the discovery that we are not separate from the deeper rhythms of life at all. We are life expressing itself."

Stefanie Teitelbaum

"Sometimes one stops breathing. It just seems to happen. I stop breathing, as patient and/or analyst, singer, walker, swimmer, and beyond. I remember being coached and coaxed to breathe in childbirth. I sometimes have to re-mind, or re-psyche myself to breathe. It's a gap more often than a catastrophe these days. It used to be the other way around.

"I sometimes notice myself breathing regularly when the patient stops. Sometimes the patient joins me, sometimes I stop and join the patient. Interesting to think of a breathing container in the background to support the gaps. And the not-breathing container too. A rhythm of collapse and recovery through a vertex of breath, no-breath."

Mitchel Becker

"In Hebrew, crisis, supply, and birth have the same root. In Greek myth, plenty and empty begot love."

Keri Cohen

"I imagine crisis, supply and birth to come together somewhere between 'now–here' and 'elsewhere.'"

Greg Pierce

"I think sometimes that there is only one feeling—we can call it love if we like. And all the other experiences we call feelings are love in different conditions and disguises. In the context of injury, for example—maybe anger is how love feels about the other when we are injured. Maybe rage is how love feels about the other when our injury is life-threatening. Sorrow is how love feels about *us* when we are injured. Grief is how love feels about *us* when the injury is life-threatening. Or in the context of healing—maybe joy is how love feels about us when we are healing/healed. Ecstasy is how love feels about us when the healing is life-giving."

Greg Pierce again

"White light entering a glass prism and, depending on what (molecules, angles?) it strikes, splinters out into the color spectrum. The white light is love or God or what some call the 'feeling of existence'—the source we may catch a glimpse of if we keep our attention from racing away just as we awaken. So the prism is the world and fate and all manner of struggle and victory and defeat and injury and healing and the madness of the interplay of it all—and trumpets of color come blazing out to the stars, 'our feelings,' segregated and angled this way and that by the whirlwind of life."

Bonita Sutin

"Among retirement gifts after a career devoted to science, my husband, Norman, was given a very large and beautiful prism which casts rainbows for us in unexpected shapes most every morning. It is regularly breathtaking, the white light dispersed into color. Norman makes sure I know that even this distribution of colors, wavelengths visible to the human eye, is but an extremely small part of the electromagnetic spectrum with its range from low-energy microwaves and radio waves to high energy X-rays and gamma rays. In the same way, we were thinking that experience in awareness can be but an infinitesimal part of what may be 'really' happening.

"A small boy at a clinic (and this really happened) was asked by the intake psychiatrist, 'Is your mother cold and rejecting or is she warm or loving?' 'I don't know,' he answered, 'She's the only mother I ever had.'"

The only mother I ever had. The only world we ever lived in.

Bonita Sutin again

Bonita Sutin adds a quote from Thich Naht Hanh: "We have more possibilities available in each moment than we realize."

She recalls Greg Pierce's words: "I think sometimes that there is only one feeling—we can call it love if we like." And

Hafiz: "I know the way you can get when you have not had a drink of Love." And lines from Sufi poets, including Ibn Arabi and Hafiz: "Love is an ocean that has no shore."

She kindly included something I said about Bion's O, a notation for unknown ultimate reality, in psychoanalysis especially emotional reality: "When I write (think of) O, I erase the line."

The strange, embracing use of O in Bion's work, which I sometimes play with: One, Omega, Origin, Oh, Orgasm ... O.

* * *

Destructiveness is one of the great gap fillers of human life. You might say destruction creates a more visible gap, where you can see some of the results of your actions. At least in murder you get to feel your actions have some effect. Maybe not the effect you hoped for, since killing is not a lasting cure.

Ironic that Freud's id turns out to be two great modes of escape (sex and aggression) from something we may have no name for. Bion calls it nameless dread. Something that can't be filled or emptied. You may have your own vocabulary for a nameless gap.

* * *

Destruction is located at the place where omnipotence touches reality. Omnipotence destroys reality and reality destroys omnipotence.

A saving gap can forestall destruction and turn the situation into something creative. There are saving gaps and destructive gaps as well as saving and destructive containers.

* * *

Louisa Putnam

"When Luke first became psychotic, I completely stopped remembering my dreams. I was living often in a nightmare,

43

terrified of what might happen. I hid most of that from others except a very few in early years, so much terror mixed with guilt and shame. I didn't want it to be what it became, a tragedy.

"Last night I dreamt of Luke again and though I only remember a hint, the fragrance of his presence, I woke happier having passed through 'the hidden gate to eternity' and returned."

The profound absence of a lost child. The word *gap* pales when confronted with grief of such an abyss. A gap of helplessness in face of everything tried. Yet a dream brings the fragrance of his presence, a fragrance beyond the gap, passing through the hidden gate to eternity and returning with thanks.

* * *

Some kill themselves because inordinate grandiosity can't let them settle for being a person, persecuted for who they aren't rather than appreciated for who they are. Internal self-rejection is simply too strong.

Some kill themselves because the pain of living is simply too much to bear. What meaning can life have in face of so much pain? What's the sense of living?

Some kill themselves because of an unknown gravitational pull. Perhaps approaching some of Freud's depictions of a death drive. Ferenczi believed one of the mother's functions was to offset the infant's/child's death drive in favor of the life drive. That is, the mother was to offset a gravitational pull or undertow that undercuts life. Often this works well enough, never perfectly, but there are times when the pull towards death is too great and nothing one does can offset it (Eigen, 1996).

There is a story in the Upanishads about a young man who had to seek death in order to learn the truth of life. He could not let go this quest and persisted until he, indeed, met Death in Death's kingdom. They dialogued for some time, many truths conveyed. Death satisfied the young man's hunger and sent

44

him back to his anxious father, worried for his son's life. Death released the seeker, letting him know it was time to return to life, blessing him for the courage and tenacity of his faith. Two of the boons bestowed on the youth included destiny to meet good happenings together with capacity to appreciate and enjoy them.

One can view this story as a successful youthful truth journey—a necessary meeting with the Ultimate, as far as one can go. A frightening, needed archetypal journey, an ideal journey worked out in unpredictable, personal terms. A journey that often goes wrong, aborts, partly fails, sometimes disastrously. Part of the challenge is to develop appreciation for the possible in face of the Impossible.

As so often in wisdom tales, diverse tendencies are portrayed. In this case, a need to learn and meet the truth of death, which in many becomes an unstoppable vortex. A climactic moment is reached, then a reversal, carrying one back to life with renewed vision. A rebirth rhythm at the heart of life can abort and never be totally fulfilled. Resurrection through repetition, slight changes occur in little ways throughout a day, variations in aliveness–deadness that dramatic images like resurrection express. One learns to settle for partial births tinged with partial deaths or partial deaths tinged with partial births, or succumb to the Impossible Unbearable (Eigen, 1996).

The case of Ellen West opens other possibilities (Eigen, 1986). Ellen West, diagnosed as schizophrenic, was in traditional psychoanalysis for many years. Her parents felt she was not being helped enough and brought her to Ludwig Binswanger in Switzerland, whom they heard had expertise in psychosis. Binswanger interviewed her and took her on but was put off by what he felt was her infantile anger and disposition and eventually told her parents she was a hopeless case. She killed herself after his pronouncement. Carl Rogers, reviewing the case, felt Binswanger didn't or couldn't *hear* her. I think of a remark by Winnicott (1971) who said at least Freudian analysis may keep someone alive long enough for the patient to find someone who can work with madness. It appears that Ellen West's Freudian analyst enabled her to stay alive. The patient was respected and cared for while her psychosis remained intact.

This is a complex and mysterious business we live. An elderly analyst once confessed to me that when he was near the beginning of his career, a difficult patient taxed his capacity to help. He began to feel it was wrong to continue this therapy and the ethical thing to do was refer the patient to an experienced elder he looked up to. Within a year or two of this transfer, the patient killed himself. The "experienced" therapist was unable to save him. Who knows what role the rejection and transfer played or whether the difficulty experienced wasn't a necessary part of any therapy with this individual (Eigen, 1993). I have often found that a relatively younger and new therapist may be able to form a more lively and sincere relationship with a patient in need than one who has gone through the ropes. Thinking someone else can do it better can be an avoidance of going through the mess oneself. There is no rule, but I would be careful of thinking someone else can do the impossible one can't. Sometimes staying in there and staying in there some more, often years, is part of a needed test of commitment.

* * *

I would like to say a word for the freedom making room for insufficiency brings. I'm well aware how badly people can feel about themselves and their insufficiencies. But there can be a positive gain in tolerating and accepting limitations. Many people I have worked with, including myself, have felt the great relief a sense of limitation can bring.

When I was in my twenties and trying to storm the gates psychically and by writing, a voice told me that I would have to accept mortality in order to write. In part, this meant I would have to accept defects in my writing if I were going to write at

46

all. My writing would have to be something less than I wanted it to be, something less than the Great Vision.

As a young man I thought Truth could be taken by storm, by breaking through all limitations of personality, body, mind—a kind of inner commandment, thou shalt break through everything. One day, writing like mad at heightened peak and failing, a voice said I was going about it the wrong way. I should draw back, "Do what you *can*, not what you can't." The Impossible beyond remains an Eternal Allure. But on the plane of *malchut*, this life, this earth—*your* life—you must learn what you are given and what is possible (Eigen, 2014a, 2014b).

A few months later, as if to reinforce the message, I dreamt I was painting huge canvases when a dream voice told me I should paint small canvases, that I could pour my intensity into smaller spaces rather than diffuse it. I took the dream's advice and within a year my first writings began to appear.

At some point, I came upon a story Merleau-Ponty told of Cezanne. Cezanne was taken by Balzac's description of the snowiness of a white tablecloth and tried painting the snowiness he saw in his mind. After repeated failure he gave up but remained haunted by this snowiness. At some point, he decided simply to paint a white tablecloth—nothing more than a simple white tablecloth—and to his delight and surprise, "snowiness" appeared.

On my own level in my own way, I've experienced similar surprise when miracles of experience given up on appear through limits one has tolerated or embraced. Something comparable happens in many spheres, for example, problem solving. Wolfgang Koehler (1917) placed Sultan, a chimpanzee, in a challenging situation. A banana is placed high out of reach in a cage along with objects that might be used to reach it, a table, chair, separate sticks that can fit together. Sultan tries what he can and has to give up, retiring in gloom in a corner or going about his business. At some point, it all comes together as if in a flash of insight: he puts the sticks together, stands on the chair he places on the table and reaches the banana. Koehler depicts insight in terms of perception of relations. Poincaré (Ghiselin, 1985) has similar descriptions of mathematical reasoning and Ehrenzweig (1971) of artistic creation.

There are many Zen stories with a parallel structure. The Zen seeker unsuccessfully descending the mountain, failing to achieve enlightenment, returning to the life he *can* live. Or another who "gives up" and modestly tends the garden of his experience until one day, he "accidentally" stubs his toe on an obstacle that opens the gates.

Sometimes the descending movement takes a despairing turn. For example, the Sumerian proverb, "I escaped the wild ox, only to be confronted by the wild boar." Or the Zen story of ascending the mountain in a storm in which the seeker can only go as far as the next flash of lightning reveals. He waits on flash after flash to be able to climb from one wet, cold, windy place to another.

The Tower of Babel appears to be one of Bion's favorites (Eigen, 2011). People cooperate and work together building a tower to reach heaven. What could be better? God here may be a destructive force in us that can't bear the success of others, spoils constructive effort, and throws all into dispersal. A movement from cooperative communication to inability or difficulty in communication, increasing rivalry and violence. God as a violent model for problem solving. This could be viewed as the creative process in reverse or a further stage of creativity sometimes described as creative destruction. Or perhaps God is a punishing force in us because we can't be real enough and break through falsity and limits. We punish ourselves for incapacity. A powerful force of self-rejection, in part, because we cannot do what we cannot do, a force in us that tries to break through the intractable, tenuous ground in which life and death hang in the balance.

In face of a massive self-destructive tendency, tolerance, working with, appreciation of creative limits sounds better and better, if only it can be achieved. I remember how comforting it was to learn about flaws in Asian rugs becoming a creative part of the pattern. And the more than comforting, vexing, inspiring ambiguity of flaws that grace, curse, and bless patterns of our lives with vicissitudes of possibility. God is, partly, a condensation of our multiple tendencies.

* * *

DANIEL: I've been thinking about our ten years together. I came after I got sick and thought I was going to die. Why I thought therapy would help me live in face of death baffles me. Maybe I thought you'd help me die better. I know therapy helped me get through chemo with a better attitude. Treatment demolished me but I came back.

I went to the beach this weekend and had a moment I want to tell you about. I was walking with my feet in the water, then started a slow run which I could not keep up with and went back to walking, trotting for moments, mostly walking. It's impossible to say what happened. The sunlight, warmth, two low clouds that seemed almost to touch the water. I could lift my hands and bring them down. Water aglow with liquid sunlight, the purest whiteness of clouds you ever saw, blue sky never-ending. I watched my feet, ripples as they moved, one after the other, the touch of water around them. I couldn't believe I was alive. I started crying. I never thought I'd live to feel this again. All life touched me in a moment. There was nothing more I could ask.

That night I had a dream that took me by surprise. Doctors feared that they found something awful in me. Scans showed they would have to open me and take it out. During the surgery they called others to see what they were removing. Somehow I could see too. Was it something living inside me, a bird? Something I didn't know about, malignant beyond words? I watched but did not know what I was watching. How bad was it? Was this finally to be the end?

M.E.: It almost sounds as if life and death are indistinguishable. In this case, bad follows good.

DANIEL: Beauty and horror.

M.E.: Together?

DANIEL: That's what I fear. But that is what my experience tells me. Good and bad go together. Something beautiful beyond words, something awful beyond hope.

M.E.: Is it a psychic malignancy you feel? Something bad in you? Something good, something bad?

DANIEL: Can one tell the difference when something is a feeling or physical disease? The beauty I felt during the day was real. I could not tell how real the malignancy in my dream body was. The fear is real. The beauty and fear are real. But how understand them?

* * *

Several weeks later after seeing doctors and tests ...

DANIEL: The numbers were good. Nothing growing inside me. I dodged another bullet. A friend once had a pregnancy in which some kind of mass was growing, not a baby. She felt the baby turned into a clotted mass, as if it didn't want to come into life in human form, for good reason. A refusal to be born as a human being. This touches me and makes me wonder in what ways I don't want to be born as a human being. What am I being born as? What sort of thing or being am I? What is growing inside me if it is not a physical mass? The psychic mass you were talking about? What can that be?

I was grateful that for the moment Daniel was physically all right. Once having an aggressive cancer one lives on thin ice. One lives on thin ice anyway but may not be as aware of it. He came through this episode physically intact but altered psychically. More intensely aware of the Great Beauty in life, the beauty that lifts one beyond all questions. And the Great Fear that lives inside one, that turns everything into questions. I thought of Jung, how the unconscious compensates for conscious states, providing other possibilities. In this case, beauty in the afternoon, dread at night, feeling fulfilled to feeling uprooted. Bion's examples, like the "Tower of Babble", in which a good state suddenly turns bad.

M.E.: Did the disease or threat in the dream nullify the beauty you felt that day?

DANIEL: It shook it up, it shook me up. But no. That was the point. Both are real. One doesn't nullify the other. They challenge each other, add to each other, take away from each other. You'd like it one way but they're both on the palette.

M.E.: The robe of many colors.

DANIEL: More—more than that. They are alive. Not something you wear. They live in you. They are your feelings, your insides.

M.E.: Like the bird you caught a glimpse of when the doctors opened you up?

DANIEL: Like the bird.

* * *

The malignant mass the doctors feared inside Daniel brings to mind a chapter title in *Feeling Matters* (Eigen, 2007), "Trauma Clots". So many kinds of trauma clots with different densities, power, and inertia.

Arnie, the patient in "Trauma Clots", first spoke of a relatively trauma free life. He lived near woods and water and

51

felt he had an idyllic beginning. He complained that it was too idyllic as he felt it left him weak when later his family moved north to New York City. He wished he were tougher.

Here is a good example of how we wash things and change them. Arnie's depiction of an easy life in the south scarcely took into account his mother's hospitalizations for depression, which must have been anything but easy. Perhaps the weakness he felt had sources other than easy living. A good early background scarcely explained why, in his first session with me, he announced that if he was not helped in one year he would kill himself.

I could not help associating his suicidal feelings, at least in part, with the trauma of mother loss. A loss not as clear as mother dying, a real and final happening. A loss of another sort, unexplained changes in his mother as she collapsed through herself and became a different person, losing capacity to function maternally or at all. One might call this a loss of contact with reality or being wounded by an incomprehensible change in reality. A breakdown of living as something like death swallowed his mother over and over, threatening to swallow him.

He came north for his father's job but within two years his father died and when Arnie was in college, his mother was permanently hospitalized. When he visited her in hospital she tried to entice him sexually or was semi-comatose or angry, a dreadful sight. He felt crushed by loss and deformation but had enough resilience to finish school and begin a career, surviving several breakdowns of his own. He married, supported a family, became a grandfather, lived a full life. At the same time, inside were demons.

Two demons we pinpointed were the "heh-heh devil" and the ghoul. The former was a head devil, looking on with contempt and scorn at the flaws in everyone and everything. If we could somewhat pin it down, it was located behind the eyes, perhaps a kind of third eye, a hate-filled eye-mind. The heh-heh devil was my term for the scoffer, the one above it all. At some point after the scoffer made its appearance, Arnie introduced himself as a ghoul. He would start a session repeatedly saying, "I am a ghoul, I am a ghoul," almost a chant, display, or flaunt, a showing, a communication from his insides to mine. The ghoul turned out to be an amorphous body sense, absorbent and engulfing, built around a core of malice, plea, pain, seeking nourishment devoured by blemish.

A head demon and body demon, expressing psychic functions—a cruel eye-mind and fusional–explosive body-sense, variants of Elkin's transcendental ego and body ego (Eigen, 1986; Elkin, 1972). After demarcation of this topographical territory, Arnie was able to contact what he called "dread" and "dead" spots, at first in his mother, then in himself. The ease of country life in the south was breaking down as the horror of his predicament gradually seeped in. Therapy has the chance of letting in trauma in nearly tolerable doses so that some digestive processes can occur. Clots one didn't know were there begin to break up, at least somewhat, with more psychic circulation possible. Head and body demons, together with dread and deadness, constituted a double annihilation largely outside awareness, experienced as being marred, deformed, at times monstrous. Glimpses of the inner trauma world began a movement towards a little more psychic freedom. The outside world may precipitate pleasures and pains, but internal minimisation–magnification processes respond. One carries many psychic deaths in one's search for life.

As therapy went on, the trials Arnie felt after his move to New York began to take on more coloring, not simply a matter of good before the move, bad after. Life in New York may have been more difficult in many ways—the jungle of the city. And while massive loss occurred, challenges grew in complexity and possibility. As he stumbled into his vocation,

New York provided stimulation he needed. The place in which one lives and survives provides its own specific elements for psychic growth, its special mix of nutrients and toxins that evoke capacity.

* * *

In the chapter "Words" in *Feeling Matters* (2007), I describe a moment in which consciousness mutates, an awareness of oneself dissolving. An eternal moment of watching oneself go under forever. To never stop seeing oneself ever going under.

A patient feels he remembers keeping his head above the waters as he drowned in infancy. How is that possible? To watch oneself go under, unable to let go seeing, unable to stop drowning. Seeing and drowning at the same time. An impossible state? Yet the moment I heard his description, I felt it in myself. It raised something I implicitly sensed but hadn't located, an experience that helped me with many patients since. To watch oneself drown and be truly drowned—and truly watch. A moment that goes on and on—to be always watching–drowning. One sees what is happening as one goes under. And keeps seeing and going under.

A variant of this appears in the chapter, "Election Rape," in the same book. A woman's feeling of watching herself being abused as a baby and child, unable to do anything about it. She contacts skin sensations of the happening and watches as she fades away. To never stop watching as she never stops fading away. Part of being mute—a kind of inner muteness—is disbelief that what is happening can happen. A state of internal shock stretched over a lifetime.

* * *

There are ways we are blinded by trauma. See God and die, see Medusa and turn to stone. Both positive and negative experience can be too much for us. Even glimpses can be blinding, perhaps one reason Homer is represented as blind, blinded by seeing too much. Yet humanity also insists on seeing and wisdom, something gained by noticing.

Perhaps a new kind of sight is growing, ability to see ways that trauma is aggravated by self-traumatizing processes. In *Rage* (2001b) I note that the Western canon of literature begins with war provoked by erotic theft. In this case sexual not land or property. A war that is the beginning of immense journeys reverberating to this day. The first word of Homer's epic might be translated as rage or a related affect state, of which rage is one of the most total and orgasmic.

Sometimes it takes the horror and thrill of war to notice internal violence, although war usually deflects the latter. There was a period in Arnie's therapy where he felt sadness for all the pain in the world, wept over injuries we cause each other, especially wars but also in the family. He began to have more of a sense of how his mother's deadness evoked dread in his baby being but quickly deflected to suffering humanity. He pictured baby anxiety met by mother's deadness spiraling before dulling. The felt vision was too much to take and quickly became sympathy for soldiers maimed and killed in war, or people in civilian life suffering violence, daily news horrors that inflame, also carry an unconscious message: this is inside us, not just outside. These terrible outsides are our insides made visible.

Arnie speaks of his wife's anger and unforgivable things he did to his children when they were young. At the same time, he envisions more of the dread he suffered while growing up and ways he tried to mute it, make it go away. Outside–inside meld, become images of each other, echo shared processes within ourselves and the outside world. If I were seeing him today, he might add suicide bombers within and without, and much else in contemporary machinations in face of our shared and separate plights.

Deflection is part of the way we work for good and ill. It can be part of imagining and symbol making. We have many filter systems and creative tendencies. Freud listed a host of psychological translations of physiological filters and vice versa, among them, displacement, condensation, symbolization, repression, dissociation, fusion–dispersal, rationalization, denial, projection, selection–inhibition, later elaborated by Anna Freud and others. The issue is not being without them but how we are used by them and use them—what quality of being can grow.

Arnie's case presents a sense of difficulties related to deflecting experience and the need to build tolerance for working with states like dead–dread rather than transforming them to outer realities like war, violence, reactivity, failure of responsiveness. War as a sea of deflection. How ubiquitously psyche is deflected, the war or trauma world within enacted in the outside world, perhaps in hopes it will be noticed. We have very little capacity to tolerate buildup of internal drama compared to what is needed.

An evolutionary challenge and, at this time of history perhaps a necessity, is to develop the capacity to tolerate buildup of inner experience and work with it. No simple matter. Internal and external war cannot be easily separated. Similar or overlapping processes occur in both directions. At least some of us, some of the time, can try to tolerate a little more contact with ourselves and become more observant of its workings.

* * *

Freud wrote of anabolic–catabolic tendencies in many kinds of relations, as part of every psychic act. He describes the former as building up of psychic life, the second as its breaking apart. The latter has come to have both passive and active aspects. Falling apart, a sort of psychic entropy is one, active breaking apart, breaking down another. Pierre Janet (McCurdy, 1961) emphasized a passive falling apart. Freud came to emphasize more an active breakdown, but included aspects of Janet's sense as well. Freud, too, emphasized repression, an active process, Janet dissociation, which has once more come to the fore in psychoanalysis (Eigen, 1986).

The terms link with diabolic–symbolic, the former ripping down, the latter uniting, building. As noted earlier, Bion writes a good deal about break down tendencies, for example, his depiction of the Tower of Babel story (earlier in this work and Eigen, 2011). Here the human race builds and God breaks down, as often happens in Bible stories. The destruction represented by God is also a human tendency, one that may have many functions and expresses an unsolvable (so far) problem. Later in his life Freud associated the tendency to build up with a life drive, the tendency to break down with death drive.

As mentioned before, the death drive has taken on many connotations, associated with entropy, black hole, creative destruction, a death wish, an active or passive gravitational pull towards death (zero stimulation), self-destructive tendencies. Earlier in Freud a self-destructive tendency might be an aggressive component of Eros turned against oneself. An impulse may turn outward or inward, against the other or against the self, many relations possible. Bion writes of a force that goes on working after it destroys time, space, existence, personality, feeding on destruction itself.

Flannery O'Connor (Eigen, 1998) depicts what appears to be a demonic force in personality aimed at cleaning the personality of both vice and virtue, all semblance of egocentric self-possession. Destructive cleansing, self-cleansing. Perhaps she partly had in mind the Christian transformational vision of losing yourself to find yourself. In this regard, she saw a positive function of a certain kind of violence that takes heaven by storm, total self-dedication to godliness. In her work what sometimes seems like self-destruction becomes a divine path but at other times she depicts a wholesale destructive tendency, not entirely unlike Bion's.

Much psychoanalytic practice has been aimed at ameliorating self-destructive tendencies. In some cases, good feeling offsetting bad. Often there is work with self-defeating tendencies of various degrees and levels, how one works against oneself. This is not so radical as the destructive force Bion points to or O'Connor's demonic–divine violence. Taking the edge off inner violence aims at helping people live better lives and sometimes comes under criticism insofar as it seems to embrace an "adjustment" psychology wedded to social values that need critical examination. There is the psychoanalysis of radical transformation and psychoanalysis of practical adaptation and everything between. Freud does not expect the negative force to vanish or be defeated, but as he put it, even a little shift towards life over death battalions can make a big difference.

Life–death dramas play out in many keys. In a recent play, *Detroit* by Lisa D'Amour (2011), the battleground shifts between social adaptation/failure to adapt and deeper visions and promptings of life, all of them mixtures and partly mad. We meet two couples living next door to each other for the moment. One couple with a house of their own and mortgage payments that have to be met. The other temporarily in a relative's house that, we learn later, they broke into and occupy by stealth.

The house owners, Mary and Ben, are hosting the drifters, Sharon and Ken, who are barely staying above drug addiction and dereliction. They are outdoors, backyard to backyard in the summer, Ben putting steaks on the barbecue. From the outside, harmless enough. The couples exchange confessions that they are both in need of friends and appreciate true sharing of feelings. One a hardworking couple, the husband recently laid off from his job. The other in a house with no furniture and life without financial prospects—although living in the moment, celebrating impulse. One still seeking a tottering American Dream, the other somewhere else, bordering on vagrancy.

I'll omit moment to moment permutations of exchanges as the meeting unfolds, except to say we learn Ben, too, is a dreamer. He is setting up a web business to help people with finances but spends most of his time on a fantasy site pretending to be British. We descend more and more into a whacko world that becomes hallucinatory. Ben tries to help Ken invest smartly and the latter tries to draw Ben into a wild, promiscuous night out, as the women try to go on a camping trip that aborts. The culmination is Sharon's wild vision igniting Mary's mind and the men catch the flame as well. Ken pours some kind of lighting fluid around the "responsible" couple's home and they burn it down. Soon enough we see Ben and Mary watching—enjoying in horror—the demise of what they worked so hard to build as Sharon and Ken vanish, vacating the premises. What can we say?

A life gone up in flames? A phony life based on the American Dream? Was it completely phony or even basically so? Was Ken and Sharon's life true? Were Ken and Sharon like the demon force in Flannery O'Connor that wipes out falsehood? Is that kind of truth true or another form of arrogance or incapacity? There are many ways to interpret the duality being imaged. What have-nots have and haves do not? What we all have and have not?

I'd like to focus on the tendencies to build and tear down. You see it in little children building towers with blocks, knocking them down, building some more. The image is ancient and in all religions. A force that brings life and death, health and sickness, well-being and harm. I used to hear the saying that it's better to light a candle than rage at the darkness. So many nuances go into building and burning, development and freedom.

Spiritual paths speak about becoming free from the prison of ourselves and limitations of mind, body, personality. Free from life and death, free to live and die. Gods that create and destroy, creation and destruction with myriad faces. These threads are touched in endless scenarios. Sisyphus pushing the rock up the mountain and down it comes again, like Babel or a child's blocks, over and over. One moment, apocalypse, the next utopia, death, and resurrection. And so it goes. We never stop representing it. Some lives are almost archetypal representations of the beauty and horror of destruction, the devastation that made Billie Holiday's soul-voice greater, ravaged glory that goes deep. As I've written (2004, 2011), Winnicott's work tends to represent the good after bad, Bion's the bad after good, storm–calm back and forth and fused.

To what extent is the human race glued to self-destructive urges? To what extent are the latter freeing, cleansing, creative? Freud wrote of creative–destructive aspects of every psychic act, inner–outer destruction. He put a tracer on aggressiveness as a fundamental issue for civilization. Bion emphasized we don't know what to do with our capacities. What kind of partnership with ourselves is possible? It is too easy to glorify impulse or stability. We are much more complex.

* * *

Fragment from a first session ...

LOIS: I spent my life wanting to be a writer. I wrote incessantly but published little. I was worried about myself. A worried child and a worried adult, if I can be called an adult. I'd say I worried about everything but that would not be true. I worried less about others than myself. I was and am a very self-centered person. I don't like to say it but it's true. And even while I say it I find it hard to admit. I wish it weren't true.

I run away. That's not quite true, only half of it. I seek and run. Sounds like a childhood game, only it's not a game. It's my real life. Now I'm in my sixties and my life is floating by me. Not that I haven't lived. I lived a lot and hard. Many men. I'm a good editor and supported myself OK enough. But I wish I edited my life better. After all the smoke and bells and whistles cleared, I'm all alone, friendless. More alone than ever.

Not that I don't know people. That's the point. I've known lots of people. My life's been full of people. I've always had periods of isolation but make good use of being alone. There's so much if I can get out. Movies, plays, walks, museums, music—the city is packed. It stings me that I have no one to do anything with. No one wants to be with me. I do everything alone. And aloneness of writing, my life.

Now I begin to feel writing is not enough. My life is not enough. I never used to feel that. I think it began without realizing it as friends dropped away. They were busy with their own lives, families, and work. I didn't marry. The closest I came was thirty years ago. I lived with a man two years, got pregnant, he wanted to marry me but I couldn't do it. I had an abortion and he married someone else. My best relationships were with married men. Figure that out. I was in therapy for years and figuring things out didn't change them. I don't regret most of my affairs—they heightened my life. I guess I didn't want to have children enough to—well, give myself up. That's what it felt like.

Marriage or even a long relationship with one man was too much a threat. I was afraid of not just losing myself but decimation. I saw marriage as domination and I wouldn't submit. I wanted to be myself but now I'm afraid I shortchanged myself. Isn't that an irony: shortchanging myself because I wanted to be myself.

A negative path as life preserver, a need to break things down to find myself. I look down at and envy those who can find themselves with someone else. Relationships make one feel loss more, too much for me. I'm afraid of losing what I have and even more so losing what I don't or can't have. I'm lucky to be able to take care of myself.

I've been with many therapists—like affairs with many men. Except you're the first male therapist I've had. I only had women therapists and stayed away from men, the same way I didn't want to submit to marriage and motherhood. Now, late in the game, I figure what the heck, why not try something different. The aloneness has gotten too much for me. Submission is beginning to look a little better.

M.E.: Are those the only choices?

LOIS: There's more?

M.E.: Has a difference between submission and surrender ever had meaning for you?

LOIS: They're both life threatening. They meld. I bolt. I don't want closeness, I want something real. Closeness smothers reality. I like taking things apart, seeing what's there, telling the truth.

M.E.: What kind of truth? The kind that sets you free?

LOIS: Now you're judging me, the way men do.

M.E.: You don't judge men?

LOIS: I bask in sexuality and sharing a sense of the real, see what's there. I'm very analytical. But now I'm wondering if the kind of truth I tell cuts both ways. The truth is defensive truth. It narrows feeling so I escape free.

M.E.: Free of the wound of relationship?

LOIS: When I said I was selfish I meant I wanted it to be my way.

M.E.: Or the ground opens and swallows you.

LOIS: A snake eats me.

M.E.: You are trying to escape the snake-bite?

LOIS: Trying not to get eaten.
[Long silence].

LOIS: This is the closest I've come to tears in years.

M.E.: Sometimes when I see the word "tears" I think of being torn inside.

LOIS: Yes, all torn up inside. Always trying to make it good,
          save my life at my life's expense.
          [We are quiet again. After a time, Lois wipes her eyes].
LOIS: Last night before I came here I dreamt I was in a burn-
          ing house and outside it watching it burn. I need you to
          say something, please say something.
M.E.:   Are you watching your insides burn, your life burn?
          You have had a passionate life that is leaving you cold.
          It is disappearing within you and you are watching it
          disappear.

Lois weeps and weeps. After a long time she looks at me and
we see each other, feel each other's life-feeling, inwardly touching each other for a moment.

* * *

MARK: It's weird but I'm weird. I don't know what I mean
          when I say that but I feel it inside. It comes from some-
          where I can't find. A slow wheel is turning out words
          and weird keeps coming out. There is a well inside
          and something black comes out of it. That's all I know,
          all I can see. I never told anyone, not this way. This
          thing inside that makes me feel marked. A black mark
          deep inside.
              Sometimes I fall inside the sound—weird. Trapped
          in a word. Trapped in sound. It's scary and comfort-
          ing. Somehow I feel at home in it, but it freaks me out.
          A bell inside saying, "Help, help." A gnome sticking
          its tongue out at people.
M.E.:   [So many threads to touch. For the moment, I pick
          what I think might be more accessible.] Weird as rebel?
          Your rebel self?
MARK: Yes, there's that. My fighting self. I won't be what you
          want. I won't be anything anyone wants. I feel a tight
          fist. My body becomes a tight fist. I am a tight fist. No

one can get me. I remember sticking my tongue out at people when I was little. I think it made me big. As an adult, I might translate it as "Fuck off." I wonder, is that what people who show their dicks in public feel? Look at my goodness, admire me and fuck you. In your face. Showing the badness, wanting the bad mark to heal. How bad and good I am at the same time. I'm starting to sound like a nursery rhyme ... Say something ...

M.E.: You didn't want your badness washed away by phony goodness?

MARK: Or real goodness. My bad boy self was a price I was supposed to pay for mommy's goodness. For someone to be good to me I had to make believe I wasn't bad.

M.E.: And now?

MARK: No mommy and daddy anymore, just me stuck in the adult world.

M.E.: What's a poor guy going to do?

MARK: Will therapy wash the black mark away?

M.E.: Do you want it to?

MARK: I want to feel good.

M.E.: Feel and *be* good?

MARK: Are you telling me it's impossible?

M.E.: Just wondering together ...

MARK: What about you? Do you have a black mark too?

M.E.: If I told you it is buried deep inside the human race, would you believe me? Would that be of any use to you?

MARK: All my life I've thought it was only me. I was worse than the others.

M.E.: And now?

MARK: Now I see what people do to each other and wonder.

M.E.: You've begun to notice.

64

MARK: Yes but I'm not sure what I'm noticing ...
           Something ...
M.E.:   Could a piece of it be that you are beginning to notice
           that people try to wipe out the black mark with vio-
           lence? You were afraid it would be erased by good-
           ness.
MARK: The black mark is an important part of me and it's also
           crying for help.

* * *

My secret

When I was young I looked up "eigen" in an etymological
dictionary and among its meanings found the conjoined opposites, proper-weird. At first I thought that being proper and
different were opposites that went together, two sides of a coin.
One kind of example might be Mark's good-bad boy. In Latin,
proper is associated with own, one's own, giving eigen a sense
of singular, individual.

In college I learned that the word eigen is part of the name
of shops in Germany, having to do with "my own"—my own
shop. My German gym teacher would sing a German love song
with my name in it, meaning something like my own rose. It
was the best gym class I had in college.

In my twenties, I learned of *Eigenwelt* in existential therapy
literature on *Mitwelt, Umwelt, Eigenwelt*, meaning dimensions
of social, natural (biological), and self, our own-world.

With this as part of my background, it was not surprising I
vibrated upon hearing of Marion Milner's book, *A Life of One's
Own*, her emphasis on self and own experience.

It did not take long for Mark to begin to catch on there were
two weird people in the room, two beings obsessed with singularity and the need for help and self-expression. One might
wonder or object, Did this take away from Mark's own need
for singularity, now that there were two of a kind? Another

conjecture might involve an invitation to evolve together. Is all humanity a kind of endlessly multiple Siamese twin? (Eigen, 1986, 2012). From weird to weird.

* * *

"Weird" can have many meanings. Another patient said he felt weird because he needed more time alone than his girlfriend did. She needed to socialize more and wanted him to share this with her. "She makes me feel weird because I don't need to be with people as much as she does. I need time alone to do certain things I like. She thinks it's abnormal and maybe she's right. But now that I am saying this I don't think it's so weird at all."

* * *

Lynn

"I dreamt a woman was trying to sell me a new alarm system, saying mine expired, it was time to renew. I am anxious. If I don't get it will something bad happen? Maybe I don't need a new alarm, the old one is working. I suspect she is trying to sell me something I don't need. She sits on top of the sink, her legs showing, long, sexy, stockings. She might have had high heels or was barefoot, waving a leg. What was she doing there? Alarming me? I tell her I am staying with my old alarm, my present one. It's OK, it works, it's not expired. I won't be injured by not switching. She made me feel it was imperative to switch, to change or something bad will happen.

"The sense that something bad will happen if … If I do this, if I don't do that. It's a haunting part of my life, not my whole life, but there since I was little. It gets me into trouble. I *must* change jobs, I *must* change relationships—that's the right thing to do. Re-new. Re-charge. Start fresh. I'm alarmed enough. Who is this sexy alarm woman, trying to be sexy? Is it something in me never content? And what does she offer?

66

Will my life really be better if I follow her urging? She sounds like she is trying to help me but I think she is fucking me up. I'm alarmed enough. Do I need a new alarm, another one? Or am I missing the point—she is trying to sell me something that will make my life better, a better system, one not so panicky? I am caught between. But I tell you what I really feel: I've had enough leg waving, phony sex, phony seduction. I just want to be myself. OK, I'm alarming. I alarm myself. Just being alive is alarming. Life is alarming. What do I do now?

"You know, I don't have to do anything. Just sitting here with you is a good feeling. That's what I think is happening. A good feeling is seeping in, alarming my alarm, calming me a little. It feels good to sit with you, to try to say it like it is, to just be. I feel a little better when I'm here. Is something urging me to leave, find another therapist, turn us upside down? Go from one alarm to another. Other therapists have told me there's nothing scarier than a good feeling."

* * *

Bion supervised a case in which he felt the patient was afraid that her urge to exist would kill her. In fact, his first wife died in childbirth and one of this patient's fears was giving birth, whether to a child or herself. Bion also spoke of taking his patient, Samuel Beckett, to a talk of Jung's to celebrate the end of their therapy. Beckett was taken with Jung talking about a patient who had never been born. It may be there are individuals so afraid of themselves or therapy that they are never born as patients, although the more radical fear is of one's own birth as a person. Lacan also mentions that if one is not born, one does not die. If we are alive we die many times. One can never be born enough but even a few times is a lot. There is much fascination with the "unborn" and for good reason. Bion, too, speaks of something in us forever embryonic. Berdyaev writes of "neonic" freedom, by which he means something neonatal in human existence. He has in mind, especially, spiritual possibilities. We are speaking of an area in which births of any kind have risks and lack of birth also has its risks.

Susan Deri told this story a number of times during the last seven years of her life. I heard her tell it at seminars and meetings with Bion, James Grotstein, Edrita Fried, and Sylvano Arieti. It was as if she had to keep telling it, perhaps out of guilt or wonder or perplexity, sharing, showing, asking. I think of Theodore Reik's compulsion to confess. I heard it in my early forties and by the time you read this I will be an octogenarian.

Her patient's diagnosis in those days was chronic schizophrenia, which meant low expectations for cure (Eigen, 1993). Nevertheless, some remedial help was possible. Susan had helped him have his own apartment, support and take care of himself, and enjoy what pleasures were possible. It was a long therapy and he was not satisfied. He wanted to fall in love with someone who loved him. This was something Susan did not have in her own life. She feared for him. She feared he was reaching beyond himself and would be badly injured.

And then one day it happened. He fell in love with a woman who loved him. His heart burst with happiness. Susan was happy for him but fearful, circumspect, uncertain. They married within the year and on their honeymoon he drowned, a heart attack while swimming in the ocean.

* * *

We learn to dampen the intensity of life so that we can survive life. A balance between aliveness–deadness is repeatedly renegotiated (Eigen, 1996). Some people get addicted to high intensity and become self-indulgent. Some adapt downward and feel a lonely, deprived lack. There is a wide spectrum of possibilities. As a human group we are not sure how to modulate our life and death feelings, a perennial challenge, and try to make the best of what we can, trial and error and, hopefully, learn from experience and example as we go along.

There are mild, mid–low-range moments of grace that seem to exact little price and in their own ways, offer much reward, little bits of grace, embarrassingly simple. In the morning I was on the dead side and began coming to a little after noon. It was my day to cook dinner and on the way to the store noticed new chalk or paint lines drawn on the road, improvised pedestrian passageways. Neighbors took it into their own hands to draw pedestrian walk lines on busy corners, an attempt to slow traffic that often speeds by. I guess I caught the spirit. As I came to the first busy crossway I saw someone unable to make up her mind whether to go or stop, so I slowed my car to a crawl, waved her on, and her face lit up and sent me a smile.

I enjoyed the moment for its own sake but having the kind of mind I do couldn't resist thinking about the importance of slowing down for others (and yourself!). Something my neighbors care about too and it already bore fruit.

Two blocks later, at a major crossing, the traffic light was changing and a man running to beat it suddenly stopped cold and rocked back and forth, vacillating, should he, shouldn't he—again, I waved to him and he lit up, smiled, waved back and went. I wasn't in a hurry and look what a little graciousness can do.

The mood continued checking out of the food co-op. A young woman behind the cash register looked glum, kind of zombie-like. I said a few words, asked if she was OK. Slowly, then with a slight startle, she came to life, filled out, our eyes met. She looked surprised and happy to make human contact and when I left saw she was engaged with the woman at the register next to her. Little nothings and the day feels differently.

I remember a moment when a therapist at the end of our first session said, "Have a nice week." No therapist had said this to me before. I left with a glow.

* * *

How could such a surface remark have so deep an effect? Have a nice week. The words went through my being like sunlight. Through deep, dark places with little access, offsetting a pull towards self-loathing. Is that possible? It happened in instants and is still happening five decades later. A good word that doesn't stop. It added to my awareness of the battle inside between good and bad feeling, love and self-hate.

No end to depth, surface part of it.

As a child there was a taboo against the depths. My mother would caution, "It's not good to go too deep. You'll open Pandora's box." In almost the same breath I'd hear about the children starving in childhood, I'd better eat up. When I exasperated her she might say, "Go dig a hole to China." Sometimes I would picture digging my way through the earth and meeting someone digging their way from the opposite direction and we'd accidentally meet.

We sometimes speak of surface and depth as meeting, as if the two are separate. One thing we can do with each other is to help create links between capacities. The taboo against the depths seems to be part of a domain that severs links between capacities. Therapy offers a unique distillation of a capacity at work in everyday life, possibilities of bringing dissociated states together, in this case a simple good word that went ringing through the psyche. One result is a persistent wish to help others in similar ways.

* * *

I'm often asked how did I manage to write so many books. I would have been content with one or two and never dreamt of the outpouring that happened since the age of fifty, thirty years ago. If you are reading this it is probably my twenty-sixth book. I couldn't have written any of them before getting married and I couldn't get married before Wilfred R. Bion told me to when I was forty-one. Within four years of our meeting I married and became a father, something I had wanted to do since my twenties (Eigen, 2014c; Eigen & Govrin, 2007).

Writing has been part of my life since childhood but has had a long evolution. Several of my literature teachers in college spotted and predicted it but I was largely baffled by their observation. An unexpected detour into psychotherapy, which became a lifelong journey, became my material and set the writer free.

I was once on a panel with Joyce McDougall who, after she finished speaking, turned to me and said, "Now it's your turn to sing." Writing is indeed a singing, an urge to express the feel of life, psyche, soul, spirit. An appreciation. One could call it other things, exploration, study, re-search, drive for discovery. But at bottom it is a falling in love with something mysterious, an act of intimacy, drawing close to psychic life.

* * *

All my books are deeply wounded. I used to be perfectionistic and paralyzed. Accepting the mortal wound opens the soul's mouth (or music, dance, art, philosophy—depending on one's bent). An amazing outcome is that what you feared and thought you gave up shines through. Whether Kali, Ein Sof, dread, beauty, hearts of thorn, the thing itself, O, a touch of heaven, hell and everyday life—the wondrous, living moment.

There are tales of people bargaining their souls for a miniscule fragment of such a gift. It is free of charge, grace. But much goes into it. William Blake writes of a moment in each day that Satan cannot find:

There is a Moment in each Day that Satan cannot find
Nor can his Watch Fiends find it, but the Industrious find

71

> This Moment & it multiply, & when it once is found
> It Renovates every Moment of the Day if rightly placed.

(Milton, 35: 42–45)

In the same poem Blake writes of a moment less than the pulsation of an artery in which a poet's work is done and great events of time conceived.

We could get lost in the associative work of Blake's vision and getting lost would be a journey through worlds of mind. Here I am selecting a limited thread, neglecting wide fields of possibilities. Satan and hell can play a positive role in creativity. For one thing, Satan is associated with energy which the voice of the Devil calls "eternal delight." "Energy is from the body" and "Man has no Body distinct from his Soul; for that call'd Body is a portion of Soul discern'd by the five Senses, the chief inlets of Soul in this age" (*The Marriage of Heaven and Hell*).

Blake's vision uses dualities to leap beyond them. Jesus is Imagination, essentially poetic imagination, which is existence itself. We may get stuck in one or another state and turn these states into beliefs we fight over. Imagination travels between and beyond any state. For Blake, "all states are eternal" and further experience is possible. Imagination opens faith and faith opens Imagination, tastes of inner freedom and Grace.

Sometimes I find myself saying, "I believe in moments." Whether successful or not, my work is devoted to living moments. Sometimes I liken my work to "Where's Waldo?" Can you find the sentence or phrase that touches the place you need touched?

Bion spoke about finding a living spark in a session. So much might seem to be dead, detritus, vacuous, waste, but buried in the session may be sparks of life needing to be fanned. Winnicott, too, spoke about nurturing a vital spark, as does Kabbalah. As a young man I was lifted by Winnicott's vital spark and his style of communicating a profound faith and feel for experience. I felt, too, Bion transmitting it ever more brightly near the end of his life. Here is a brief excerpt from one of his last talks (unpublished), 1978, London: "Can one look at all this debris (of a patient's life), and detect in it some little spark still … of life, which could then be fostered or developed in a way which could lead to *rejuvenation*, as we call it … of the whole personality?"

* * *

Freedom has many meanings. It can apply to different qualities of duration. Some moments feel freer than others. A baseball player makes a great catch and says it all came together in an instant, a moment of freedom. One moment a dancer feels freedom of movement, another stiff and awkward and tied up. At the beginning of one of my books I wrote something like, "The big lie is that we are going to live forever; the big truth is we are living forever now." Hyperbole, to be sure, yet something is being communicated, a domain not exhausted or done justice to with terms like "free will."

When the Zohar says, "There is a rose and there is a Rose!" it differentiates between states of being, a less and more inspired state, a less and more inspired life. Bergson's, Poincaré's, or Bion's emphasis on intuition takes us beyond "willfulness" to a creative place that opens, uplifts, excites, casts down, envisions another kind of experience.

Terms like "good or bad will" express an attitude, temperament, or sensibility that go beyond "willing." Language offers phrases like "good and bad heart," as if we have two hearts, a good and evil will or inclination that is more or other than will. H. Niebuhr (1941) writes of good and evil imagination as a background for what ordinarily is meant by will. Minds can be more or less inflamed, as in inflammation or inspiration. Think of all the meanings of the word "fire" when it comes to human emotion, from Eternal Flame to hell. Saint Paul says better to marry than burn in the hell of passion. Gratification can open heavens that deprivation can't.

So much can be said about experience in the goal region. Each state contributes.

In my teens I thought Milton wrote *Paradise Lost* when a blind old man. I would picture a feeble, old man speaking his poetry to his daughters. It took some refocusing to realize he finished his first draft in his late fifties and died about seven years later, the same age Bach did. To the eighty-year-old man writing these words, sixty-five does not seem as old as they did to the teenager. Yet even to the teen *Paradise Lost* meant a kind of freedom. Not freedom of will but of word and meaning, vision, imagination, faith. The depth of description and expression, nuances of states so easily recognized once seen. What words can do, lighting matches in the dark and making worlds visible. More, when I read Rilke I felt he created experience as he wrote. When I read the word "well" in the Bible, I think of this well within without end.

When Bion spoke in New York (1977), he recited whole swaths of *Paradise Lost* at a party given to honor him. I was in the small group around him at the time and felt instantaneous release, permission. If he could be him, I could be me. It was an experience I had several times in my life with different people. Upon meeting them, one becomes freer.

* * *

In my days playing jazz, I met Charlie Haden before he became known as the great bass player he was. If my memory is correct, he eventually replaced Ray Brown as the number one Downbeat poll bassist. When I met him he was kicking a heroin habit. He, Shep Meyers (jazz pianist, arranger), and I drove from Los Angeles to San Francisco before parting ways.

On the way to San Francisco, I no longer know where, we stopped at a mansion where a well-known pianist was living. We took turns playing with Charlie and at some point the well-known pianist, a wisdom figure to us, said, "Charlie, to make it you'll have to play at a high level more consistently.

You can't drop down and rise up the way you do. Your great moments are great, but you need more consistency to play with us." He meant high caliber gigs and musicians.

It was a sobering moment. He saw Charlie's potential. We felt Charlie's spark. He had the fire. But his playing was too uneven to make big time. He played wholly by ear, by feel. It was direct transmission—his insides played the bass. One could feel his inner being plucking the strings, strings of spirit. His feel for jazz had something spiritual. When he was young he sang and later played bass with his parents on a radio show. I've heard the show described as rock and folk, but Charlie said they sang spirituals, church songs too, and I could feel Amazing Grace in his playing.

As Charlie matured, he was one of the few who linked personhood with music-hood. His bass mediated the vital spark, his to yours. It's not just the music but the soul coming through the music. Bass strings, soul strings. Even in the days when I knew him, before Charlie became Charlie, his bass had a big sound that runs through you, almost pure spirit. Many years later I took my teenage bassist son to hear him at a club in New York. My son's jaw dropped, mesmerized by someone who had become himself. Charlie was caring and friendly and for a year afterwards I thought my son looked a little like him when he played, absorbing something, making it his own. Not that Charlie was without serious difficulties, as all of us, but spirit shines through them. Charlie and Shep are gone but tasted fully the experience of living spark to spark and the nightly chance of one igniting the other.

* * *

Bass and drums go together in jazz, play off, against, with, over and under each other, adhering to traditional and creating new rhythmic possibilities on the moment. Drums may be more ancient but I wouldn't bet on it, since bass, too, in its way, mimics the feel of heart beat, pulse, breathing. Think of all the forms of drumming you know, from military discipline to pulsing frenzy, big drums, small drums, and odds and ends percussionists find. One of my sons created a little drum set out of cans of various shapes and sizes before he had a traditional drum set. When he was gestating in the womb, I crazily took my wife to a Taiko concert, Japanese big drums, filling the universe with sound. The fetus crazily thumped and bounced and later became a drummer.

I love what happened to jazz drumming, the freeing up of rhythm and possibility, one move playing off another, at times light as feathers, sparkling, tickling, laughing, crying, rhythms never heard before. In college I would love it when a job was over and our drummer would put away his sticks and brushes and play for us with his hands. The rhythms seemed to make life come alive, come into existence moment to moment. I never wanted it to stop.

* * *

Among the many reasons for writing is giving expression to sparks and/or bringing the latter to life. The rhythms of words pulsate, the sounds of words create colors. Writing, too, can be a form of therapy. Psychoanalysis is often characterized as a "talking cure." Freud's use of the spoken word brings out and deepens much about speaking that is taken for granted, not noticed, or implicitly felt and assumed. At the same time, psychoanalysis can be a "writing cure." Spontaneous writing played a large role in Freud's discovery and formulation of psychoanalysis, writing as an act of discovery. The use of the word "cure" is largely poetic license, although writing can, in certain instances, play an important role in healing and opening barriers.

Writing is an act of intimacy. It is one of the amazing qualities of written communication that it speaks to people across the ages. A poet writing her heart out two thousand years ago can light hearts now. We connect across millennia. We are still digesting thoughts sent to us from people we will never see or know, from times long gone yet with us in some form. Writing takes many forms and has many uses, including sharing feeling, thoughts, states, vision. One of the places life speaks to me and others is through writing. Shared thoughts and visions across the ages can lift, enrich, open. Writing enables one to draw closer to oneself and others, insides to insides.

Bion writes about psychoanalytic writing:

> The criteria for a psychoanalytic paper are that it should stimulate in the reader the emotional experience that the writer intends, that its power to stimulate should be durable, and that the emotional experience thus stimulated should be an accurate representation of the psychoanalytic experience that stimulated the writer in the first place. (1965, p. 32)

One might pick points to quarrel over, but one gets the essential emphasis on transmission of significant emotional experience from being to being through writing. In this case, emotional experience important to living a life and, to use a Bion notation, the O of life.

* * *

One moment the O of writing portrays light, one moment darkness. What do Allen Ginsberg's *Howl* and Wilfred Bion's *A Memoir of the Future* have in common? Both portray a shriek of existence. Ginsberg tells us the best minds of his generation were consumed by madness. Bion portrays aspects of madness that permeate the human condition. *Memoir* is a kind of extended shriek, howl, or big bang of the psyche as it comes into existence or is evacuated. He amplifies psychoanalysis by showing ways one tries to get rid of the psyche because of pain it brings. A challenge is to suffer birth and development of psychic life rather than escape it and add to its pain by inflicting more pain on ourselves and others.

Bion evokes moments of implosive–explosive shatter stretched over time. Not only faith, catastrophe links personality together. A catastrophic sense colors existence. How to build resources in face of incapacity for psychic work? Psychoanalysis is one attempt to do so. To what extent is it up to the task?

To what extent do we turn to stone, go up in flames, dissolve, fragment, shatter when trying to face ourselves? What can we look at, feel, and live?

So much writing celebrates life in face of problems. Aristotle's entelechy, actualization of potential, Spinoza's conatus, Nietzsche's will to power, Bergson's élan vital, Freud's life drive, Bion's urge to exist—to name some way stations. Here are affirmations of a push towards existence, self-perpetuating movement that can turn against itself.

A lot of experiential fish swim through the nets of these drives or movements. Nietzsche portrays an Apollonian as well as Dionysian dimension. Domains of peace are contrasted with turbulence. Winnicott notes an area of quietude, calm, rest as well as upheaval and excitement. In Elizabethan literature an idealized picture of bucolic life was contrasted with the rush and busyness of cities. Explorations of peace and turmoil add to experience. Heidegger writes of *aleithea* as a clearing in which truth appears, joining peace and disruption. For therapy, this may mean an opening in which new reality is experienced or something familiar experienced in new ways. A lot goes on outside as well as within categories we develop.

Kabbalah teaches that wherever one finds oneself there are sparks to be mined, released, woven into the fabric of one's life. Psychoanalysis is a kind of embryonic spark needing nurture and one kind of psychoanalytic writing carries within it an experience of the x described, to some degree enabling the ongoing birth of psychoanalysis itself.

* * *

One could substitute whatever therapy works for you in the last sentence. Therapy is about birth and failures of birth. We are born all life long.

Bernice

"I was a mystic as a child. I could see things others didn't, spirits and mysterious presences. I saw the whole world on fire. When my grandmother was institutionalized I feared I would be too. She would sit, stare, say strange things. I would try to hear them and wonder what they meant. 'She's ill,' my mother said. Would I end up sitting and staring and speaking incomprehensibly? Would I be put away?

"I had a hard time in school. What was going on? What were they saying, the other children and teacher. They seemed to understand each other. I began to grapple with the possibility of many forms of incomprehensibility, not just my grandmother's. It began to dawn on me—I couldn't have been more than five or six—that there are different languages. Everyone was speaking English, but not the same way, not the same English. There's school language, home language, playground language, grandmother language.

"I prayed to God and God told me to learn all the languages I could but never lose my own. God kicked me into the world and said he would help me get along. It was like being born again, going to school, new worlds, new births. I was bewildered, dumbfounded but God whispered in my ear, 'Go and learn. Learning is good.' This was a lot to carry around at five and six but I felt I was being helped by an unseen helper. Did everyone have this help? My grandmother? What happened to her help? Seeing what happened to her made me wary. I grew up feeling I didn't want that to happen to me. Yet I had to take in that more was happening to me than my mother or teacher knew.

"I didn't want the fire to burn me up. At an early age I knew I wanted to live. I would have to learn languages other children used. I would have to learn school language. It was important or I could sink like my grandmother, fade out or go up in flames.

"I felt my secret relationship with God made me see the whole world more clearly. By my teens I could say there are many worlds and I was trying to navigate them. Something was determined to survive and it survived by getting born through different worlds. Now I can say my mystic self heightened my sense of reality. Realities. Your writings speak to me and I thought of coming to see if some of what I held in myself so long could meet another person."

* * *

What made it possible for Bernice to survive and develop in different worlds and over the years discover mystic and everyday realities enhancing each other? It could have gone differently, one tearing the other apart. In her case, the inner helper actually helped and did not make life impossible, as too often happens. She learned to value worlds of experience that often war with each other.

We usually look for sources of nourishment in the environment that could enable this. Spitz (1965) wrote of emotional marasmus of infants in institutionalized care, where physical needs were taken care of but emotional needs were insufficiently met. The infants not only failed to thrive but important capacities failed to develop and some infants wasted away and perished. Nevertheless, there were infants who did well enough and went on developing and living. I don't know that it is always possible to account for such individual differences, although we guess (better genes, environmental luck, something unknown).

I've long been interested in the co-constitution of self and other, which I sometimes write self–other, including a sense of generativeness arising from an implicit sense of self–other (Eigen, 1986, 1992, 2015). While ultrasensitive to self–other interweaving, there is also a "monadic" part of me, akin to Winnicott's incommunicado core. How can we be totally monadic and totally interweaving? That is one of the mysteries of our being, multiple tendencies working together in often unfathomable ways.

Balint (1968) wrote of an area of creativity as a one-body relationship, meaning one's relationship to oneself. As noted before, existential psychoanalysis distinguished *Umwelt*, *Mitwelt*, *Eigenwelt*, aspects of existence related to nature and biology, social life, and one's relation to one's own self. There are, too, authors who have written on an autistic dimension of experience, not simply as a diagnostic category but a dimension that is part of life. We have many attitudes and tendencies, expressed as diagnostic categories and descriptions, like psychopath, schizoid, hysteric, paranoid, and autistic. All states and tendencies are of real consequence for living, potentially enriching if used well. How to become better partners with our capacities is something with which we keep grappling.

Something in Bernice determined not to fall through the crack her grandmother did while, at the same time, not losing treasured gifts and possibilities. We hear advice about making the best of what life gives and what you have or can do, but there is no life without risk or danger. Where did Bernice find the resources to do what she could? Her explanation: God. But she also was aware that she pulled herself up through something that we may not have a word for.

There are many who do not have this capacity or who are unable to locate or use it. We have many myths and stories about destruction barely averted and others in which destruction occurs. In the Bible there are tales of nearly complete destruction in which a good seed survives (barely). Mythology is preoccupied with creative–destructive relations, reflecting tendencies of our beings and experiences in our lives.

One of the most famous is the near "sacrifice" of Isaac by his father, Abraham (Eigen, 2005). Murder is averted by a hair's breadth. There are believers who might say it is not murder if God ordered it; it is a sacred act. Here we are near or in a widespread realm of madness. Many sacred texts condone and even advocate holy murders, sacrifices, punishments. Don't commit murder but kill those who break the Sabbath, commit adultery or other abominations. What is the difference between God telling Abraham to sacrifice his son and God telling a "psychotic" person to jump in front of a subway train or kill his brother if he wants to save himself and the world?

Ancient literature put tracers on matricide, fratricide, infanticide, patricide and psychoanalysis has done its best to mine them. One can hardly say enough about these themes and their intrapsychic and social–political importance (e.g., sacrificing our children's blood and well-being for the "good" of the state, forms of international blood sacrifice in the name of the sacred on the one hand, survival, dignity, or power on the other).

Where did Bernice find resources to sidestep the fate of life turning against itself, catch on, and begin to learn to work with our multilingual psyche? Her visionary feel for the complexity and value of experience seemed almost, at times, at the forefront of evolution.

* * *

In psychosis (Eigen, 1986), eyes or ears may be emphasized, as in seeing and hearing things others don't. Lower body areas can also be used in hallucinatory ways as well. An individual may feel a need to shit or piss on you and the whole world or on himself. Intense urges to defecate or urinate can act as links that unite and distance. It is an intimate thing to shit on another person but, overall, quite distancing as well.

Leah came to sessions unkempt and smelly, making it unpleasant to be in the room with her. She spoke many times about being unwanted by her mother, who unsuccessfully tried aborting her. "I should be dead. I should never have been born." Unfathomable pain I dare not mollify. Perhaps I wishfully imagined that dedication to being with her would have a long-term effect.

Although she was unkempt and smelly, she was not without life. She did not entirely perish as an infant or child. She is here with me seeking herself, seeking life, perhaps driven by desperation. I imagined her parenting must have been mixed and uneven, not all bad. But that may be a psychotherapy superstition: She must have gotten something if she is here. The fact that her mother told her she was unwanted lodged in her and did not budge.

When we got into things I was able to ask if she was testing to see if I would want her no matter how unwanted she made herself, or was she unaware of her state. She said she just slipped into not taking care of herself. Her mother didn't want her, she didn't want herself.

M.E.: Were you hoping I would tolerate you, want to be with you?

LEAH: I was hoping you could help me.

M.E.: Help you how?

LEAH: I don't know myself. Make it better. Make it better.

M.E.: Make you feel better?

LEAH: Not just feel better. Be better. Make everything better. You think this is bad? You should have seen me a few years ago. I couldn't get out of bed. I got fatter and fatter. I looked horrible. Yet I had a thought that someone would love me. I knew no one would. But I pictured being loved.

M.E.: You mean if someone loved you it would have to be for yourself alone.

LEAH: Yes. There were so many barriers. For myself alone.

M.E.: Where is this self?

LEAH: It is inside me. No one can see it.

M.E.: Can you see it?

LEAH: No one can. I can feel it. I see it somehow. I don't know how but I do.

I wondered, is this wish to be seen and accepted for oneself alone a hallucination? A hallucinatory wish or searing reality, the most real thing one may feel? I pictured years ahead of us, slowly finding ways into the wish to be wanted and what living a life might mean. Are both feeling absolutely wanted and unwanted hallucinatory or important parts of larger realities?

* * *

On another side of the spectrum, in *Coming Through the Whirlwind* (Eigen, 1992) half the book is about an attractive woman, Cynthia, who slept with ministers of churches she attended. She was drawn to spiritual leaders of her communities and made use of being naturally appealing. Whereas with Leah, a challenge was working with an aversive tendency, here one worked with attraction. I could feel the pull in sessions and had to maintain the tension of affirming sexuality while engaging with what her psyche was trying to accomplish with it, the extra load it carried as an ego machine, and perhaps making up for earlier levels of nursing deficiencies, including intense withholding and overstimulation. While Leah tended to organize herself around a sense of repulsion, even being repulsed by herself, Cynthia was charged with attraction. I looked forward to the end of sessions when we touched hands goodbye, an electric thrill.

There is tension built into therapy that is unavoidable, whether aversion–attraction or something else entirely. With

Cynthia, sexual urges are affirmed in therapy without acting them out literally. But that is no different than withstanding the pull of sexual urges in raising children, affirming their life feeling while respecting their persons. It is part of a frustration built into life, a sacrifice we willingly make for a greater good. Winnicott (1992) brings this out in his "use of object" formulation (see also Eigen, 1993), where the parent affirms the infant's urge to life without allowing herself to be hurt. It is a tension built into experience which, if grown into well enough through time and repetition, promotes one's psychic growth and growth as a fuller person.

* * *

Winnicott's picture of healing involves creating conditions for a valued sense of continuity of being to grow. Gaps, disruption, disillusion, discontinuity are part of the process. We might say discontinuity ↔ continuity run through each other and enter multiple relations, oscillating, fused, antagonistic, parallel. Still, for Winnicott, a basic sense of continuity grows to encompass them, as mixed tendencies develop in varied ways.

The therapist triggers a taste of unconscious boundless support, a generative boundless unknown accessed through the medium of a somewhat known personality. A continuity that survives discontinuity, perhaps not immediately, but in time, replenishing, returning. Winnicott does not, as is fashionable, idealize discontinuity. If anything, he might idealize continuity, but it is within an overarching experience of the continuity of being, as core and background support, embracing disruption, that aloneness seeks the riches of life.

Winnicott (Eigen, 2004, 2011) tends to emphasize a moment of recovery from disruption, even madness; Bion sketches bad moments following good. With him, we enter the fall, rupture, crack (common language· uses this for madness). He is drawn to psychotic processes, which Winnicott increasingly emphasized as well. Both were influenced by Melanie Klein who focused on psychotic anxieties. Winnicott was supervised and Bion analyzed by her. They went their own ways, but would not have explored regions they did without her.

Earlier I wrote of watching oneself go under. Bion is especially sensitive to this kind of process, observing mad aspects of personality as one undergoes them. In one or another way, experiencing–observing madness was an ongoing state he kept saying more about, a reporter from the front lines. He spoke of psychotic aspects of the self and worked with patients who manifested them. If Freud spoke of working from unconscious to unconscious, Bion spoke of working from psychosis to psychosis. A kind of hallucinosis in the therapist was sensitive to hallucinatory subtleties in the patient.

To dip (or more) into psychotic processes and try to communicate, share, write them, is a gift, unwanted or wanted, that some have more than others. To see what is happening and explore it is perhaps one thing that sets Bion off from someone more fully in the grips of psychosis and overwhelmed by it. The latter rarely is able to study and explore what is happening but, at the time, is trapped. In a way, Bion is a proxy, an alter ego teaching by example, evoking a capacity to explore with respect and care processes that threaten to drown, even destroy one. One path of help is enabling your partner to be able to see and begin to explore what otherwise could destroy a person.

Winnicott appears to have great faith in evoking creative tendencies in face of destructive urges. He is sensitive to everything that can go wrong, but also tries to tune in to inherent creativeness in life. Bion calls Faith (his capital F) the psychoanalytic attitude, a radical openness in face of unknown and perhaps unknowable psychic reality. He is also sensitive to beauty:

It is very important to be aware that you may never be satisfied with your analytic career if you feel you are restricted to what is narrowly called a "scientific" approach. You will have to be able to have a chance of feeling that an interpretation you give is a beautiful one, or that you get a beautiful response from the patient. This aesthetic element of beauty makes a very difficult situation tolerable. It is so important to dare to think or feel whatever you do think or feel, never mind how un-scientific it is.

(Bion, 1978, Paris seminar)

* * *

Beauty is the heart of the Kabbalah Tree of Life (Eigen, 2012, appendix). It is the center of the tree like the heart is almost the center of the human body. The left arm is Gevurah (strength, judgment, severity, fear), the right arm Chesed (mercy, love, compassion). The two add to and temper each other, coordinating capacities, as two hands work together. They also go beyond coordination and working together, they interact, interweave, forming something new, as in chemical reactions. The "new" is placed in the middle, the center, Tiferet (beauty). It is beautiful when capacities work together and create something new, a kind of implicit model of birth, creativity. Too often capacities war with each other, dependent on the attitude that frames them.

Buddhism and Greek philosophy emphasized a middle way, harmony, balance. It is an idea that has been with us a long time. In life extreme and middle states both contribute to the pool of experience, play important roles, adding color, possibility, nuance, creativeness depending on how we partner them. In Winnicott's (1992; Eigen, 1993, 2009) writing, for example, you will find him valuing extreme states and transitional areas between. How to get along with, tolerate, use and develop the range of capacities that gift us is more than

87

a lifelong challenge, not only for individuals but the human race.

Tensions between mercy and judgment run through Robert Frost's poetry, reflecting theological disputes through the ages. Fear and love of God is an important psychological–spiritual binary. To say judgment and mercy spawn beauty is a mystery. To complicate matters, like a hologram, all capacities on the Tree of Life are in each other. There is instantaneous communication of all parts of the spiritual universe (Teilhard de Chardin's "noosphere"). There is gevurah in chesed and chesed in gevurah (like yin in yang and yang in yin). The two may seem dissociated at times but are indissolubly linked (Eigen, 2011, 2012).

There are many ways of approaching the link between judgment and mercy through beauty. There is the beauty of reconciling capacities that can turn against each other. Working together is beautiful. Conflict is part of life. How we approach conflict is critical. To what extent is creative rather than destructive conflict possible?

In addition to reconciliation, one can speak of interpenetration of opposites, an image of intense interweaving that can lead to deep growth. Different language systems developed in face of the pressure of many capacities and states they engender. Scientists speak of beautiful solutions to problems, an aesthetic element in thinking as well as feeling and sensing. In the Kabbalah tree of capacities, beauty has a special, unifying aspect as the heart's center radiating in all directions.

By inference, beauty is the heart of psychoanalysis. Perhaps there is more than one heart, but beauty is in the brew, as Bion suggests in the quote above. That Bion said he used the Kabbalah as a framework for psychoanalysis indicates a central role for beauty (Eigen, 2012, 2014c). It was in fact the beauty I felt on hearing a depth psychologist's dream interpretation when I was in college that opened the door to psychoanalysis and the larger therapy world for me. It rang a bell that keeps on ringing. Beauty as heart's center—an important part of it. The beauty of psychoanalysis has uplifted my life, enriching and opening it over sixty years. Mystics speak of intimate beauty beyond conception. I suspect many vocations participate in this beauty in their own way.

* * *

A class member noted that when people fight they most often throw punches at the mouth, an effort he felt is counterproductive, since it can bloody your knuckles and even lead to broken fingers or hand. Yet he feels a kind of attraction to the mouth and wonders about it and asked what my thoughts might be.

Besides a tendency to injure ourselves as well as others (aggression against self and/or other), I wondered about the mouth as an early experiential organ, among other things a discriminatory gateway for what gets in or not (e.g., swallowing or spitting out). Mouth is also a vehicle of expressive sound, from screams of distress and agony to coos of bliss, spectrums of affective nuances. Elkin (1972) distinguishes a transcendental ego rooted in eyes and body ego with mouth as one of its roots, a paradoxical relation between eye-mind/mouth-mind.

A neurologist I once consulted for a case (Eigen, 1986), when examining the patient's eyes with a light, said the eyes are an extension of the brain and give information about the latter. The mouth may be more tied with the autonomic nervous system, heart, and gut minds. The mouth is also involved with language and there is growing eye–hand–mouth coordination, a nexus of sensing–feeling–imaging–thinking, so things are complex indeed.

There is research suggesting a baby smiles at mother at a distance by two or three months. There are many kinds of smiles.

The distance smile can be triggered by a representation of eyes and mouth. Elkin postulates a kind of paradoxical sense, seeing the mother who has been a holding–feeding mother close (skin to skin) now at a distance, the closeness–distance paradox triggering a smile of recognition. The one close is the same as the one far away.

Closeness–distance remains a basic rhythmic pattern one grows and develops with all life long. Baby eventually coordinates seeing, reaching, taking, putting in one's mouth, the latter, in part, a cognitive organ, evaluating taste and feel, a gateway for what is taken in or rejected. In–out is a broad psycho-organismic set of tendencies that links many functions. At one point, one may link the other's face with one's own, at another a mystery of difference, same but different.

My student's question about punching the face, especially mouth? Instinctively going for a primal source of towards-away, cognition, experience, part of core aliveness, a center of different kinds of consciousness? A primal as well as practical gesture.

* * *

When a therapist works with rage, she usually tends to look for fear and hurt as background. I suspect that from infancy on one tries to offset fear with anger. Anger, too, is often a spontaneous reaction to pain, as in stubbing one's toe and getting mad at oneself. It is not just pain one reacts to, but fragility, fault, mishap, being at a loss rather than in control. One is not master of one's universe but a small ship tossed by a big sea.

Nevertheless, I would not count out a destructive tendency that can exploit rage for its own sake or other "reasons." As I've written, rage can be one of the most total experiences with its own orgasmic element, at times in the service of pleasure, intimidation, domination, and power. Lautréamont's (2004) *Maldoror* explores evil intentionality. Bion's (1965, p. 101) formulation of a force that destroys time, space, existence and continues feeding on itself after destroying everything it can destroy, Freud's force against recovery, and Melanie Klein's destructive force within (Eigen, 1996, 2004, 2007) are strong formulations of a self-destructive tendency.

One could speak of a circle, a nexus of possibility. A favored formulation by many therapists today seems to be that rage is a response to fear or pain, therefore defensive, reactive, secondary. That's almost like saying if there were no fear or pain there would be no rage. However, such a world is not one we inhabit. Melanie Klein's formulation seems the opposite. She tends to see anxiety as a response to an inherent destructive urge. One could put a double arrow between these two formulations, rage as a response to fear, fear as a response to rage, destructiveness in response to fear–pain and fear–pain in response to destructiveness. Movement of psychic tendencies is multidirectional.

In the Bible, God gets enraged by poor behavior and tries to blot out the mess he created, as in the flood. One could say the flood that nearly wiped out everyone and everything was an emotional flood, at once affirming and wiping oneself out at the same time.

The phrase "wiping oneself out" reminds me of a supervisory group in which Hymen Spotnitz (1908–2008) told a well-meaning therapist, "You're trying to feed your patient when his diaper needs changing."

At times, I feel groups and nations shit on each other, wipe their ass with each other, inflammations of mutual destruction. Can one really put one's finger on where it starts? As a group, we create myths of origin incorporating creative–destructive spirals, trying to funnel the latter into causal thinking.

I mentioned the play, *Detroit*, as a recent work preoccupied with destruction. There are many others. Woody Allen's movie, *Irrational Man*, has a man commit a "just" murder in order to feel alive, only to end up falling down an elevator shaft, an accident of his own making. The word fall is a loaded one, commingling mythic fall with real life experience as soon as one tries to walk, and likely before, since parents play with infants in ways mimicking flying and falling, high–low, up–down.

Another is Richard Maxwell's play, *Isolde*, in which a woman undertakes to build a dream house, which seems to fade as a real possibility as her mind fades. Neither aliveness of sex with the architect she hires nor the steady love of her husband, the contractor, can stem increasing loss of herself, which goes through phases: failure of memory, a sense of something always missing, a sense of disappearing, and finally, "I don't exist." One can try to blame this deterioration on empty capitalism and success, banality of married life, insufficiency of Eros, parenting, social groups, human makeup going back to and before Adam and Eve, or simple physiological deterioration, but another, more haunting sense comes through, having to do with a nameless process intrinsic to life, psyche, soul, and spirit.

One wonders about a link between emptying mind, self, personality in face of overstimulation, too much. I think of Wordsworth's words, "getting and spending, we lay waste our powers." Bion speaks of a need for space unsaturated by meaning for meaning to grow. In recent years I've seen more young people who could not finish college, could not hand in papers, or force themselves to do the needed work. It was as if their systems folded up, semi-collapsed under the pressure and demands. Something in them could not, would not. At the same time, more adults in the workforce came in with difficulties resembling chronic fatigue syndrome, their systems in a sit-down strike, forcing time off from hyper-life and business as usual. The energy and organization they needed to drive themselves disappeared.

The play I wrote about above, *Isolde*, was supposedly related to Wagner's *Tristan and Isolde*, in which lovers perish. An association between Eros and death is ancient, going back to Homer and likely before. Romeo and Juliet is archetypal. One of the most beautiful expressions of the love–death theme I know is the movie, *Black Orpheus*, in which death follows the lovers to their end, followed by dawn, children, new life, and music. Loss of personality in erotic fusion may be a dimension of the death portrayed, fulfillment that is annihilation. One of the most beautiful suicides in a movie I saw—I don't remember its name—was Brigitte Bardot gracefully, slowly floating in the air as she fell from window or roof towards the ground, a human feather transcending gravity as it drew her down. A moment expressing more than love–death, as personality disappears in its own image.

Themes of emptiness–plenitude and void–chaos are ancient and take many forms, part of spiritual as well as secular language. Lose yourself to find yourself. And the modern addition, you have to have a self to lose. My cup runneth over. Moments in Gide, Camus, Kafka, Beckett, and others portray a kind of empty loss of values, self, meaning, at times as ways of engaging the unknown. Freud's dialectic between strange (uncanny)–familiar touches this, as well as his letting the horse lead the rider, opening to creative unconscious processes. As mentioned earlier, Bion wrote of the psychoanalytic attitude (echoing Freud's free-floating attention and free association) as Faith, an attitudinal discipline of being without memory, expectation, understanding, or desire, open to O. At times, the analyst's state of "hallucinosis," a kind of blank film, is imprinted by a patient's hallucinations, developing images and intuitions, psychosis to psychosis. In one or another way, emptiness–fullness has been a constant conjunction in cultural experience with physical, emotional, and spiritual counterparts.

* * *

Psychopathy is one way we keep ourselves alive. The term has been replaced by sociopathy, emphasizing a social problem or deficit, lack of social feeling or use of social feeling to get one's way. Both terms have value. I use the old term, as I like its emphasis on individual vs. world or, in Cleckley's (1950) phrase, "mask of sanity." Defective conscience is often thought of as part of psychopathic structure, lack of concern for hurt one causes and, at times, delight in outsmarting others, their pain signifying one's superiority.

Winnicott thought delinquents experienced early gratification that they lost. It is a tribute to their life drive that they seek what they imagine will be good for them even if it is destructive. The combination of angry pain at loss fused with memory of earlier fulfillment fuels actions meant to get (recapture) the good, often at expense to others and themselves. The biblical story of the fall from Eden and murder and destruction that follows is an archetypal example. The struggle between creativeness–destructiveness continues. Cain, the killer, becomes a builder of cities.

A semi-related attitude often is part of psychopathy: If I'm to get something in life I have to take it myself because no one will give it to me. In one Zen story, villagers catch the local thief and bring him to the Zen master. The sage tells the villagers to carefully tie the man with rope, dangle him from a tree without hurting him, and bring him everything he wants. It is part of therapy lore that someone adapted to emotional toxins may lack tolerance for more nourishing fare, a capacity therapy may help to build.

There is mild–harsh, low–high psychopathy, spectrums of possibility. There is stealing and there is *stealing*, minor and major crime and violation. One would hardly call many peccadillos in daily life psychopathic. Selfish acts at the expense of others are part of existence. However, if one looks closely one can see structural similarities between me-first or us-first even if it hurts you in large and small, less or more violent situations (as often happens, both doer and done to suffer injury). Once one begins to see it, psychopathy in everyday life seems almost ubiquitous. It remains an unsolved problem of our makeup, self-affirmation with destructive components.

A famous saying by Rabbi Hillel: "If I am not for myself, who will be? If I'm only for myself, what am I? If not now, when?" Psychoanalysis tries to trace movements from self-centeredness to concern for others. Winnicott speaks of an infant's ruthlessness when it comes to getting what he needs, and goes on to try to trace development of concern, especially about damage one causes or imagines. Fairbairn proposes that some infants feel that love is damaging (Eigen, 1999, 2001a). The fate of destructive urges is a basic theme in early psychoanalytic literature and continues today. The matter is endlessly complex, since caring–uncaring, love–hate, creative–destructive tendencies are so mixed. We have predator, victim, practical, affectionate sides of our personality. Sometimes emphasis on one or another can be extreme.

A particularly confusing aspect of psychopathy involves the play of impulse and calculation. On the one hand, strong impulses are working but they may be subject to long-term calculation. A dramatic example is the way a serial killer insinuates himself into his victim, a kind of paralyzing mind control (Espy, 2015). One wonders how widespread this capacity to enter the mind or soul of the other for one's own purpose is. Bertrand Russell spoke about how patient he could be trying to seduce a woman, often planning years before the final conquest. Impulse? Calculation? There are many ways the two go together.

Invading Iraq because we were attacked by terrorists from Saudi Arabia—to flex muscles, show power, control oil, make a mark, have a strong presence? Did it help? Create a bigger mess? Heads of government seemed determined to do something to appear strong, whatever the justness or practicality of the move, a gambit many paid for with their lives. The problems and dangers in the Middle East are worse today.

I can't help linking the impulse to show strength in high places to street violence when a gang member feels dissed (disrespected), high and low psychopathy, so to speak. I once met a man who felt he could make anyone do anything he wanted. He was sure of it, absolute certainty. He must have had some successes because disconfirmation had no effect on his unbendable conviction. I wondered if there were people in high places with something of this attitude, dangers to the world operating from a position of imaginary omnipotence–omniscience.

People in the financial world speak of making a "killing." A CEO I met had a sign on his desk, "Never feel sorry", another, "No Pity". Young people on the street kill each other over drug deals. And what of economic violence within and between nations?

In earlier years of psychoanalysis there used to be the belief that you can only work with people who were accessible to psychological truth. There was back patting about psychoanalytic love of truth, yet awareness how defensive and self-deceptive we all are. Being analyzed as part of training and re-analysis throughout one's life was expected. We have to be on guard with ourselves. There was a conviction that you couldn't psychoanalyze a liar.

My own feeling was if you can't psychoanalyze a liar, you can't analyze anyone, since the one doing the analyzing is also a liar. Bion felt lying is ubiquitous but that should not stop us. Truth in one or another form is ubiquitous too. Both play roles in our lives and sometimes are indistinguishable.

There are times that truth kills and lies save. Illusion plays an important role in survival, creativity, and development. Our minds tend to simplify towards rigid categories that deform or reduce the richness of experience. What we call truth can turn out to be a lie and vice versa, depending on hosts of circumstances, understanding, growth of meaning, and perspective.

The opposite also holds. Truth saves and lies poison. Much depends on how a psychic act functions, changing valences over time and from moment to moment. One moment Jesus says to a disciple, now you are of God, and the next moment says to the same man, get thee behind me Satan, reversible reversals depending on the spirit or attitude at hand. In *Coming Through the Whirlwind* (1992) I wrote of a psychologist who used truth as a weapon. Through years of work he came to see how he used truth to wound others and distance them. Bion speaks of truth–compassion and truth–cruelty. In a parallel context, Ingrid Bergman was frustrated with a role she could not understand or feel. She was of the conviction that she would have to truly feel the heart of the character to play her. When she cried to the director, Alfred Hitchcock, about her difficulty, he looked at her and simply said, "Ingrid, fake it." It was a releasing moment for her, a satori. In an instant a wall dissolved and released her from a narrow sense of herself, a moment that grew over the years.

Too often we make too rigid a distinction between fact and fiction. When I was younger I was a hungry reader of novels. I felt novels were teaching me about life and how to live. They were essential in my learning process. The truth of fiction helped enrich and open my being. A sociology teacher in graduate school liked to say, "There's no such thing as an un-interpreted fact." Whether or not that is literally true, it brought home a sense of the creative–destructive role the mind plays in what and how we experience. Socrates taught that much of what passed for truth in human discourse was opinion, that is, fiction, mixtures of truth–fiction. He was put to death for his unmasking activity. His assertion of ignorance (I know I don't know) is part of the background of Bion's therapeutic method of not knowing, depicting the psychoanalytic attitude as Faith, a category beyond wars between psychological functions. I sense in Bion a supportive, compassionate attitude, openness to exploring the human condition, interest in rather than condemnation of the human psyche and its workings. Extended and intermittent meeting oneself.

* * *

One reason I feel we should not discount the possibility of therapy with psychopathy is that response capacity grows. We are often able to do more with psychosis than once was possible. If a man like Schreber (1903; Freud, 1911c; Eigen, 1986, 1993) walked into our office or hospital speaking about soul murder, many of us would not blink. We have a feel for what he may mean and are able to respond. A few decades ago, patients we called "borderline" baffled us. Their hostile heightened sensitivity challenged the limits of therapy. Now we have competing schools that meet with more success than before. I once learned of a species of baby bird pecking the mother's neck in a certain place to stimulate a mothering response. I think the borderline's sensitive anger forced our response capacity to grow.

At this moment of history, psychopathy is so prevalent that societies of the world need treatment. Will the pain of the world reach a point when response to it must grow? There is a huge psychopathic streak in the economic world and other social sectors. Psychopathic use of technology is accelerating. There are examples of individuals "getting away with murder" in high places, making others feel stupid for playing by the rules. It is not unusual for ethics to mask psychopathy. A patient who spoke most about being ethical and moral was the one who left without paying her bill.

I suspect many therapists are already making inroads working with psychopathic aspects of personality. Whether or not the needed response capacity is growing fast enough to help society is another question. When talking about Macbeth's question to Lady Macbeth's physician, "Canst not though minister to a mind diseased?", Bion answered, "Not now. But come back in two hundred years and we'll see what we can do."

* * *

Holden Caulfield, in Salinger's *Catcher in the Rye*, saw the adult world as phony. That is not too unusual a perception. Jesus called the Pharisees hypocrites and felt the heart of a prostitute real ("she loved much"). He spoke for the poor and said, in a saying rippling to this day, that the poor in spirit will be first in the kingdom of heaven. An inversion that works as a model for aspects of psychoanalysis, which emphasizes that which has been left out, repressed, dissociated. If Holden Caulfield saw the outside adult world as phony, Freud emphasized individual self-deception, lies one lives by. There is a long tradition in human culture charting ways we fool ourselves to get by, self-deception running through ages.

It is easy to take sides for truth against lies but realities are more difficult and thinking one's truth is *the* truth is not truthful. In couples work people often bludgeon each other with their "truths."

One man who kept flattening his wife with her perceived weaknesses finally began to see how "truths" flew from him like bullets from a gun. And it was not unusual for him to turn the gun against himself, addicted as he was to self-attack, the double directionality of aggression.

Another, after a long silence, suddenly said, "My God! I'm a fraud. We're all frauds. We're making the whole thing up. My whole personality is made up." Far from this being a condemnation, it was a moment of self-transcendence, a freeing moment. Instead of coming down on himself he felt compassion for his predicament, humankind as a whole. It was a moment of inclusive self-love, inclusive of all of us, not without humor. There is biting wit and humor, satire, irony, ridicule and that has value, like acid rubbing off corrosion. But this man's tone was more a meld of humor and kindness tinged with forgiveness. I felt my heart tear up and smile. It's as if, for a time, he stepped out of the iron maiden that encased him.

This was in contrast with a man who was encased in playing or being God without knowing or caring about it. He scathingly dressed down his wife and played on her sense of truth about herself. What he said hit home but in a way she could not do anything about. He castigated her for failing to be the picture of the woman he wanted in his mind. His wrath was unmitigated and she withdrew until the storm passed. They had many good moments and were bonded by children and the fullness of life at other times. He rationalized his rages as justified. She could not argue about some of the content but the delivery was devastating.

It was enlightening to link his outbreaks with the use of the term righteous in religion. There is an uplifting, aspiring use, to be holy, pious, a better person. But there also is a wider spread sense of self-justification, feeling right and the other wrong, being the purveyor of godly truth, one's own ego or self as godly dispenser of justice. One day he came in with a dream in which God, as in the story of Noah, decided to obliterate the universe. Its evil was intolerable. Then the tone of the dream abruptly changed, like an actor stepping out of character, speaking directly to the audience. A voice said calmly, "All the rain is your rage." He woke seeing the rage of his being raining on his wife and she cowering, trying to take cover until it was over.

He came to session quaking, almost cowering in fear of himself. He thought of his wife and children and cried, "I want to change. I don't know how. Please help me." "It will be hard. It will take time," I said but felt a difference, something happening. I thought of Scrooge waking up the morning after prophetic visitations, glad he had another chance. At that moment I felt time is everything, and as the man wept I did too. It is not easy to give up being God and become, more fully, a human being.

* * *

Many therapists feel a sacred element in their work. Bion explicitly finds Faith underlying psychoanalytic encounter, feels it to be the psychoanalytic attitude. In *The Electrified Tightrope* (1993, pp. 277–278) I write, "In this business we deal with broken lives and heartbreak, and we do so with our own broken hearts. Yet we discover, within our patients and ourselves, heart within heart within heart. What a breathtaking experience to discover such richness at the null point, always more than we can take."

Rabbi Nachman (Eigen, 2012, Chapter Two) said, "Nothing is more whole than a broken heart." He told his students to speak to God from their hearts in whatever language was most natural or no language at all, a cry from the heart. At the center of the heart is a smile of joy and cry of sorrow.

Rabbi Nachman also spoke of profound stillness in the center of our beings and demonstrated by dancing. It is said his dance had such deep stillness you could not see him move.

In psychoanalysis, Frances Tustin (1995) wrote of heartbreak at the center of existence. She was writing about autism and childhood psychosis and black holes of separation, but her work has far-reaching implications and touches implicit aspects of the human condition.

Some find ways of being nourished by this heartbreak and it becomes creative heartbreak. Some are crushed, destructive heartbreak. Some do not survive. It is a terrible thread in life yet can be raw material, stimulus for growth. One of my heroes in my twenties, D. T. Suzuki, wrote that loss of his father at the age of six and a brother the following year stimulated his spiritual quest for a father substitute. When he studied away from home he felt a need to return to his village to see his mother, sometimes walking many miles for a glimpse of her.

Her death when he was twenty-one enforced separation. At some point, he received an assignment to go to America to help with translations and write about Zen. He felt he could do a good job academically but did not achieve sufficient satori for deeper authenticity. Every morning he sat at the zendo trying to give all he could to his meditation. At last came a point where he felt better equipped to undertake the task, which became a central part of his life work, adding to his growth.

Martin Buber, another influence in my youth, whose writings Bion valued in old age, wrote about the breakup of his parents' marriage when he was three. He did not see his mother again for several decades and then only once, what he felt was a miscarried meeting. He was raised by his father's parents.

Before the early breakup, he remembers a feeling "of certainty that nothing could happen to me" (1967, p. 21). It is a feeling my wife and I sometimes joke about when we are feeling too good. A paradigm: "I really feel good. Haven't been sick in a long time." Followed by getting sick, as if the good feeling was a harbinger of illness on the way. Here, for young Buber, a sense of invincibility, nothing can go wrong. And then his world falls apart.

When his mother left he was sure she would soon return. A year later, an older girl who took care of him, told him his mother would never come back. He felt freed by a sense of truth. Someone finally told him the truth and he recognized it immediately. From that time on the words "cleaved" to his heart and in ten years transformed into a sense that this cleavage was true not only of him but humankind, a rupture in the human soul. At some point, he coined the word *"Vergegnung"*, "mismeeting", "misencounter" as an expression of failed meeting between people.

Buber was so invested in a sense of contrast between real and false meetings that he wrote (1923) "All real living is meeting." He acknowledged that much of life was spent in many states, some far from I–You realness. He spoke of a melancholy passing of You to It, as states change and operational–instrumental needs become paramount. In a touching few sentences Buber sketches the one time his mother visited him after leaving in childhood. By that time he was married with children. He recognized the beauty in her eyes but felt the meeting empty. As they were together, an inner voice formed the word, "*Vergegnung*," a defining moment that heightened the value of real meeting.

* * *

I hope I did not imply that Suzuki or Buber reached a stasis of self-definition in search of their paths. Buber was suicidal in his teens and recounts an important turning point in his forties. A student unexpectedly sought personal time with him one night when Buber was studying and writing. Buber turned him away, impatient not to disrupt his own meditation. The young man killed himself and Buber quickened in realization: That young man could have been himself, in some way was himself. To deny the appeal of the other because one could not be bothered was unconscionable, a kind of costly replay of his mother leaving him. He denied the other as she denied him, centered on her own life, a pattern alive beneath all words and philosophy. The experience, played out at the cost of a life, heightened his dedication to the importance of meeting, a life and death matter. His failure prompted him to say that a man does not mature before his fifties. Maybe that's a tiny bit like the Zen artist saying his paintings did not start to come alive before his eighties. There are ways something in us comes more alive the older we get.

Suzuki's (1969) autobiographical writings are short but priceless. We learn about his background and aspects of his development and many questions remain. It does not appear he finished his Zen training or college but a life of Zen can be felt through him. I like to joke, "Look what a little Zen can do." But it was far from little.

When he did not make much progress with "one hand clapping" his koan was changed to "mu", which opened him, enough for his teacher to give him the name of Daisetz, meaning great simplicity or humility, although he liked to say it meant great stupidity. He was deeply moved by one of his teachers reading a passage about snowflakes falling, the latter phrase said repeatedly. Snowflakes falling, flakes falling … When I read his description of these moments I feel oneness of existence, all of us falling snowflakes, and something in me loosens, breathes, thrills, frees, and sometimes weeps.

He took an assignment in Chicago to help translate the Tao Te Ching, learned Chinese and Sanskrit, continued important translations and eventually began teaching and writing about Zen. I am tempted to leave out "about" and simply keep: writing Zen. There is Zen writing, as there is Zen drawing and painting and gardens. His enlightenment process continued and reached a special turn upon thinking of the line, "The elbow does not bend outward," an experience of freeing limits. Things fell into place, capacity to work with reality. I often heard the term "creative limits," working with what you have and are and can be, learning to use materials you work with, finding the possible. It is a relief to discover you can be.

For a "simple" man, life could get pretty complicated. He taught in England, the United States, Japan and had multiple homes and wives, a Japanese wife who raised his children, an American wife who taught with him and fostered his writing. I have not been able to find out what happened with his children. It appears he lived most of his life away from them, as he had been fatherless from an early age. A few years after his American wife died, he became close with a Japanese American student in one of his Columbia University classes "… who, as his secretary, companion and intimate friend never left his side for the rest of his life. Through her he gave us articles, books and worldwide correspondence; with her young life to help him he lived, I am sure, just so many years longer" (Humphreys in Suzuki, 1969, p. xv).

* * *

Suzuki and Buber both turned to spirituality and philosophy in face of traumatic loss, Bion to psychoanalysis with profound mystical, philosophical currents. Love of nature played an important role for Suzuki and Bion. Each of these men's sensitivity spanned many dimensions. Buber was very much impressed by his father's feeling for nature. All had profound love of wisdom and a sense of the present moment.

It is a mystery how wounds and scars give rise to creativity and/or do us in. Some show their wounds by inflicting pain on others, in some cases, mass destruction. As if by killing or injuring others one kills or injures the wound in oneself. Others share great wounds of humankind in their work, uplifting life and spirit.

* * *

Our personalities are very mixed and while we diagnose ourselves in terms of categories there is much fluidity between, within, underneath, to the side of what appear to be rigid organizations. One can be psychopathic and sincere at the same time. On the face of it, such a statement is unacceptable to our wish for neatness. Reality feeds and challenges our viewpoints.

I've seen individuals who need to injure, outwit, and triumph over others while at the same time feeling seeds of devotion. A man who loved his daughter, nevertheless, felt justified in abusing her. At times he thought that through his sexual initiations he was raising her to another level. He lacked a sense of the damage he was causing or didn't care, feeling justified by the surge of his own feeling. A woman told me that a man

105

who raped her kept saying how soft she was and that he felt her love for him. Although some who injure don't care how the other feels or even relish the power of injury, others positively imagine or hallucinate complicit states and appreciation. In a recent war, leaders told their troops they would be greeted as liberators, whereas their reception was much muddier, seared with endless conflict. Our minds are, partly, propaganda and self-propaganda machines, capable of idealizing acts of murder.

What leads to what often surprises. Bion celebrates the grave thieves at Ur, who drilled through rock at just the right place to enter the queen's chambers 200 years after internment. They also drilled through the prevailing dread of spirits who were certain to seek revenge. Bion felt a monument should be erected in their honor, as early scientists braving the feared unknown. He applauded a positive value of greed in search of discovering riches and knowledge. Today we may speak of greed gone wild in the amazing financial octopus that grips the world.

* * *

No human being ever lived without pain.

That may be so of all life forms. I imagine plants feeling pain when they are broken, cooked, or chewed. But could we live without them?

Judaism seeks to raise the level of killing life for food by blessings. It is rationalized: animals and plants are made for food and we elevate them by blessing them and being nourished by them. One could go to an extreme and say they fulfill themselves through us.

Cavemen did the same by painting animals they depended on, investing them with sacral beauty. This capacity to make murder sacred for the sake of life applies to many areas of social existence, war, for example. If we look at animal sacrifice of ancient times as primitive, what should we call the sacrifice of human life for tribal survival, grievance, and power? Human egocentricity is boundless. So are sacrificial needs.

And the still, small voice within? Is it only or mainly a voice, or a felt sense that fills existence?

Since pre-antiquity I imagine some quota of pain has been associated with spirits. The holes in brains of cavemen might attempt to let the bad thing out, a predecessor of brain intervention to alleviate mental distress. The rat chewing an injured limb makes me think how we eat our insides, causing more pain trying to end it. We eat our insides eating us.

One amazing quality we possess or that possesses us is the ability to ask unanswerable questions. Wittgenstein noted that language creates questions and ways of thinking that take us quite far from realities of life. He spoke of language games, varied ways of organizing experience. How language is used became a focus. He felt many metaphysical concerns would disappear with better use of language. Yet Wittgenstein had a strong spiritual sense, wordless and with words. Buddha has some commonality with Wittgenstein. When asked questions like is the self eternal, does it exist after death, and so on, he said we cannot know. Just keep practicing. Stay on the path, your path, your practice. There are many ways to say this. In the Bible, God asks, "Where are you?" And mortals answer, "Here I am." Find where you are and practice. In some sense, one practices existence like a musician practices an instrument. One may stumble on depths without end.

We ask questions about pain that cannot be answered. Yet something happens when we focus on it in therapy, spiritual practice, and by touching our lives through time and growth. Therapy work is not easy. Pain is part of it. So is love. For some, love is the greatest pain of all.

Husserl and Bion distinguish between thoughts and thinking thoughts. A thought can appear but can you think it, work with it, let it develop and bring it to various fruitions? Feelings come but can we work with them, link with them, let them develop, and let them develop us? Bion speaks of pain and suffering pain. The latter is more a process of experiencing experience, letting what you feel work on you and with you and you it. Growing together, partnering each other.

One may wonder if for us there is such a thing as a purely physical pain and what that may mean. We are psychical beings, feeling beings, experiencing beings, psycho-physical, psychophysicalspiritual. Fechner, the creator of psychophysics, turned to experimental work to try to trace interactions of body and spirit, partly owing to recovery from his own psychotic states. A unifying vision of spirit and matter was part of his cure. It was from Fechner Freud got the phrase: "the other scene," meaning dreams and the unconscious (Eigen, 1986, Chapter One).

Pain we have is felt by someone, a psychical being who relates to it with imaginings, knowing, feeling, worry. Pain hurts yet there are many ways to experience hurt. One could apply the Husserl–Bion thread to many things. One's own life, for example. It's one thing to be alive, another to live it. One thing to have a thought, another to think it. One thing to have a feeling or sensation, another to feel or sense them.

Many simply cannot endure existence and, tragically, end it. The same pains that may kill someone may be a creative seed for another. For some, it is both. A discovery I made in my twenties by accident—I could easily have perished—is that by going into my pain, the pain of life, and further into it, and further, a miracle can happen. It perforates and opens other worlds. I think this is not for everyone all the time. It is often good to distract yourself or another away from the pain and towards something neutral or pleasant, like one might a child. But there are times a child needs to cry fully, I suspect to feel depths of his being, endless depths, no end to pain, no end to existence.

One thinks of great myths of suffering. Buddha going into the pain of suffering until it opens to nirvana, samsara–nirvana as gateways. Jesus transforms death into Life. Chuang–Tzu has a moment where he says, "There is only Life." He says this in face of great suffering.

To some degree, therapy, meditation, prayer, and life are experiments in practicing. Even when helped by another, you are practicing to see what works for you. The process does not stop.

We are playing with fire. There come moments when what works for you only works for you, your spark, your Daemon. What form does your practice take at such moments? It may take a lifetime to find out and as the end draws nearer one is still practicing and finding out.

REFERENCES

Balint, M. (1968). *The Basic Fault*. London: Tavistock.

Bergson, H. (1911). *Creative Evolution*. A. Mitchell (Trans.). New York: Cosimo, 2005.

Bion, W. R. (1965). *Transformations*. London: Karnac, 1984.

Bion, W. R. (1970). *Attention and Interpretation*. London: Karnac, 1984.

Bion, W. R. (1978). Paris seminar. F. Bion (Ed.). http://www. psychoanalysis.org.uk/bion78.htm.

Bion, W. R. (1994). *Cogitations*. London: Karnac.

Buber, M. (1923). *I and Thou*. W. Kaufman (Trans.). New York: Touchstone/Simon & Schuster, 1994.

Buber, M. (1967). *Meetings*. London: Routledge, 2002.

Cleckley, H. (1950). *The Mask of Sanity*. Louisville, KY: Presbyterian Publishing.

D'Amour, L. (2011). *Detroit*. New York: Faber & Faber.

Ehrenzweig, A. (1971). *The Hidden Order of Art*. Los Angeles, CA: University of California Press.

Eigen, M. (1979). On the defensive use of mastery. *American Journal of Psychoanalysis, 39*: 279–282.

Eigen, M. (1983). On time and dreams. *Psychoanalytic Review, 70*: 211–220.

Eigen, M. (1986). *The Psychotic Core*. London: Karnac, 2004.

Eigen, M. (1992). *Coming Through the Whirlwind*. Wilmette, IL: Chiron Publications.

Eigen, M. (1993). *The Electrified Tightrope*. A. Phillips (Ed.). London: Karnac, 2004.

Eigen, M. (1996). *Psychic Deadness*. London: Karnac, 2004.

Eigen, M. (1999). *Toxic Nourishment*. London: Karnac.

Eigen, M. (2001a). *Damaged Bonds*. London: Karnac.

Eigen, M. (2001b). *Rage*. Middletown, CT: Wesleyan University Press.

Eigen, M. (2004). *The Sensitive Self*. Middletown, CT: Wesleyan University Press.

Eigen, M. (2005). *Emotional Storm*. Middletown, CT: Wesleyan University Press.

Eigen, M. (2007). *Feeling Matters*. London: Karnac.

Eigen, M. (2009). *Flames from the Unconscious: Trauma, Madness and Faith*. London: Karnac.

Eigen, M. (2011). *Contact with the Depths*. London: Karnac.

Eigen, M. (2012). *Kabbalah and Psychoanalysis*. London: Karnac.

Eigen, M. (2014a). *A Felt Sense: More Explorations of Psychoanalysis and Kabbalah*. London: Karnac.

Eigen, M. (2014b). *The Birth of Experience*. London: Karnac.

Eigen, M. (2014c). *Faith*. London: Karnac.

Eigen, M. (2015). *Image, Sense, Infinities, and Everyday Life*. London: Karnac.

Eigen, M., & Govrin, A. (2007). *Conversations with Michael Eigen*. London: Karnac.

Elkin, H. (1972). On selfhood and the development of ego structures in infancy. *Psychoanalytic Review, 59*: 389–416.

Espy, J. C. (2015). *There Is No Body: The Dark Boroughs of a Pedophilic Cannibal's Mind*. London: Karnac.

Freud, S. (1911c). Psycho-analytic notes on an autobiographical account of a case of paranoia (dementia paranoides) [the case of Schreber]. *S. E., 12*.

Ghiselin, B. (1985). *The Creative Process*. Los Angeles, CA: University of California Press.

Henle, M. (1962). The birth and death of ideas. In: H. Gruber, G. Terrell, & M. Wertheimer (Eds.), *Contemporary Approaches to Creative Thinking*. New York: Atherton Press.

Koehler, W. (1917). *The Mentality of Apes*. London: Routledge, 1956.

Lautréamont, Comte de (Isidore Ducasse) (2004). *Maldoror and the Complete Works of the Comte de Lautreéamont.* Lykiard, A. (Trans.). Cambridge, MA: Exact Change.

McCurdy, H. (1961). *The Personal World.* New York: Harcourt, Brace & World.

Niebuhr, H. R. (1941). *The Meaning of Revelation.* Louisville, KY: Westminster John Knox Press, 2006.

Schneerson, M. M. (1999). *The Passover Haggadah.* Y. B. Marcus (Ed.). Brooklyn, NY: Kehot Publication Society.

Schreber, D. P. (1903). *Memoirs of My Nervous Illness.* New York: New York Review of Books, 2000.

Spitz, R. (1965). *The First Year of Life.* New York: International Universities Press.

Suzuki, D. T. (1969). *The Field of Zen.* C. Humphreys (Ed.). New York: Harper & Row, 1970.

Tustin, F. (1995). *Autism and Childhood Psychosis.* London: Karnac.

Watts, A. (1989). *The Book: On the Taboo Against Knowing Who You Are.* New York: Vintage.

Wertheimer, M. (1940). A story of three days. In: R. N. Anshen (Ed.), *Freedom: Its Meaning.* New York: Harcourt, Brace.

Winnicott, D. W. (1971). *Playing and Reality.* London: Routledge, 1982.

Winnicott, D. W. (1992). *Psychoanalytic Explorations.* C. Winnicott, R. Shepherd, & M. Davis (Eds.). Cambridge, MA: Harvard University Press.

INDEX